THE
GOSPEL'S
SAVING
POWER

By

RANDY LANE BUNCH

TIMOTHY
Publishing Services

The Gospel's Saving Power
© 2013 by Randy Lane Bunch

Published by Timothy Publishing Services
3409 W Gary St
Broken Arrow, OK 74012
918-924-6246

ISBN: 978-1-940931-02-9

Library of Congress catalog card number: 2013954716

Printed in the United States of America

DEDICATION

To my late parents,
Barney and Margierie Bunch,
Who showed me the way of salvation.

CONTENTS

FOREWORD

My spiritual father once said to me that on any subject, there are people who "*think* they know, " and then there are people who "*know* they know." This is especially true when it comes to salvation. Randy Bunch has taken a biblical subject that many people—saved or not—think they know about. He then leads us very diligently through a biblical study of what "salvation" really means and its benefits. The power of the Gospel "to save," includes many elements and Randy has presented them to us with an anointing and clarity.

What a powerful book! I would encourage everyone to get this anointed book. This is a book that brings a deeper understanding of the meaning of being "saved." This book will open the eyes of the reader who is still uncertain of the meaning of salvation. It is important to study every scripture reference it cites and look up every point. By doing so, this book will move you to a point of certainty about what salvation means, and detail the many benefits that come with being saved.

As Randy and Maria's pastor, I know they have a strong desire to bring the Body of Christ into a more mature and closer walk of faith with God and other believers.

What a great job, Randy. May you be blessed and built up by the same faith you have ministered to the Body of Christ through this book.

Dr. Billy J. Rash

Senior Pastor

Kern Christian Center

ACKNOWLEDGMENTS

I believe that every book is a collaboration. Those of us who write, teach, or preach today stand on the shoulders of those have gone before and imparted to us what they learned. They have our thanks. My new collaborators, Tim McKitrick and the team at One Seed Press, have been a patient and invaluable help in making this book the best it could be. Thanks so much, Tim, to you and all your crew for the hard work.

Additionally, there are some who were particularly instrumental in helping me navigate the transition into this new season of life and ministry. My special thanks go to the following:

Pastors Ron and Regina Griffith, and the congregation of Westside Believers Fellowship, for getting me on my feet; Pastors Billy and Shelby Rash, and the congregation of Kern Christian Center for the encouragement to move forward; my dear old friends, Larry Carroll, and Kevin and Veronica Powers, for being there from the beginning; Randy Griffith and all the gang at RTI for a place to learn and make a living. There are many more who helped me in various ways. I am grateful to you all!

Thanks also to my in-laws, Ray and Donna Smith, and my stepsons, Blaine and Landon Reich, for their generous welcome into their family. A particular word of thanks to my mother-in-law for her help in checking my grammar and punctuation in this manuscript.

To my children, Charissa, Christian, Chloe, and Cameron, thank you for always loving and supporting your dad. I love you with all my heart.

Lastly, to my lovely and loving wife, Maria; I love you, and I am so grateful that we're on this journey together. The best is truly yet to come!

INTRODUCTION

Are you saved? If you were raised in church, especially in the kind of church in which I was raised, it was a question that came up a lot. We asked everybody, "Are you saved?" or "When did you get saved?" We knew what we meant, and for years as a young child I assumed everyone else knew what we meant too. I was wrong. As I've gotten older, I've realized more and more that we only knew "in part" what it meant to be *saved*.

As a young boy of six or seven, I had my "salvation experience," and I was eager to make sure my friends got theirs too. So I would ask my friends if they were saved. The question was a good one, as far as it went, but often I was misunderstood since my Christian vernacular failed to communicate to the larger world what I meant. It was, in fact, around this time that I began to realize that many people didn't have a clue what it meant to be saved in the context in which I, or my church, meant it.

Two young friends were my first evangelistic victims. I remember asking one of them if he was saved. He seemed to actually resent the question and think it preposterous that such a thing could have happened to him.

"No, I'm not saved," he said quite emphatically. Then he turned to the kitchen and yelled out to his mother for confirmation, "Mom, am I saved?"

"Sure," she answered dryly, never taking her eyes away from the dishes or whatever chore she was doing. "Jump in the water and I'll save you."

For me it was no laughing matter. I took their sarcasm in stride, but even then I knew it was a serious question. They were nominal attendees of a local church, but had no idea what it meant to be saved.

I tried with another friend who had been raised Catholic by his very devout Catholic mother. She stepped in to answer and assured me that her son was indeed saved, and that the matter had been taken care of through his infant baptism. Again, I knew this answer fell short of the mark. At six or seven years of age, I was no theologian, but I knew that such a personal matter as one's relationship with God could not be decided for us by someone else – well-intended mothers included. No rite or ritual of the Church done *to* us, apart from our own volition, could produce the life-changing experience of salvation.

Perhaps my first realization that not everyone understood what it meant to be saved occurred the day after my own salvation. God had been dealing with my heart. The Southern Baptist church I attended in our small oil field town in Southern California was between pastors at the time, so an itinerant evangelist, Brother Bob Allen, was serving as interim pastor. We all liked him, as he was a very capable preacher. My mother told me she would have him talk to me, as I was ready to give my heart to Jesus and be saved.

Brother Bob spoke to me at Training Union, the Sunday School-like class held before the Sunday evening service. To be honest, I don't remember much of the conversation. In fact, even at the conclusion of the evening service, I had trouble answering the questions he asked me before the assembled crowd.

"Randy, what has Jesus done for you?" he asked. "Did he die for your sins?" I knew the answers but couldn't recall them at the time in front of all those people. What I *do* remember was that something happened inside me. Tears welled up in my eyes as the greatest change that can happen to a human being occurred within the sacred chambers of my heart.

While my mother nodded to Brother Bob's questions as to whether my decision met with my parent's approval, something changed forever in my life. This was over forty years ago, yet the memory of what occurred that night is still vivid. I had indeed gotten saved.

The next morning, I remember things were different somehow. I was in the second grade, and felt I just had to share with someone what had happened to me. My schoolteacher seemed to be the safest person with whom I could share my experience.

"Mrs. T_____?" I said, "I got saved last night." I guess I expected her to share in my excitement, but instead she seemed uncertain how to respond and unfamiliar with what I was talking about. To her credit, she didn't challenge me or attempt to discredit my experience. She even attempted to be encouraging. "Well," she said, "I guess everything's all right for you then, isn't it?" That was it. I affirmed that indeed it was "all right" for me and took my seat for the start of class, but even then, at that tender age, I could tell there was something different, not only with me, but between her and I. She had not understood, and I don't think it was just my terminology she failed to comprehend.

Just as my friends and my second-grade teacher didn't understand what it meant to be saved, there is a world out there that is desperately lost and dying, facing a dark and hopeless eternity unless someone intervenes. They need to be saved. They need the Savior.

Between a lost world and a loving Savior, God has placed the Church. We are called by God to be ministers of reconciliation; to herald the truths of the Gospel of salvation that the world may hear and believe and come to personally realize the immeasurable grace of God.

The question once asked in the Scriptures still rings out with the same power today as it had when it was written thousands of years ago…

How then shall they call on Him in whom they have not believed? And how shall they believe in Him of whom they have not heard? And how shall they hear without a preacher? And how shall they preach unless they are sent? As it is written: "How beautiful are the feet of those who preach the gospel of peace, who bring glad tidings of good things!" (Romans 10:14-15)

This book is written for the army of believers who must answer the need of this generation. Many people in the world are asking questions. For countless people, life has left them empty, and they are searching for meaning and a sense of purpose. Jesus said the fields are "already white for harvest" (John 4:35). It's not a matter of opportunity or demand. The demand is there and the opportunity has never been greater. The problem is one of supply, and that is where we, the Church of Jesus Christ, must step up.

Jesus said, "The harvest truly is plentiful, *but the laborers are few*" (Matthew 9:37). That has never been truer than now. We are the stewards of the Gospel of salvation to this generation. To effectively communicate this message, however, it has to be real to us. We shouldn't *communicate* what we cannot *demonstrate* as being real in our own lives.

The purpose of this book is to explore what it means to be saved; to give both the believer and the curious seeker a fuller understanding of what Christ has provided for us through God's great plan of redemption. For those who have been a little myopic, as I was for so many years, seeing only one aspect of the salvation Christ came to bring, this book may hold some unexpected surprises.

We will delve into what the word *salvation* really means and explore its multiple applications and dimensions. These discoveries will do nothing to take away from what, for many of us, was our classical understanding of salvation in the new birth. Rather, they will only serve to enlarge upon the goodness of God and give us an understanding of the broad, comprehensive provision He has made for every aspect of our lives.

Ultimately, my prayer is that, having received of His grace, you will freely impart to others what you have received. As you become a recipient of this wonderful and full salvation, may you also become a witness of the truths that have set you free; an evangelist to the lost of this world.

God is still asking, "Whom shall I send, and who will go for Us?" (Isaiah 6:8). May our answer ever be, as Isaiah's was: "Here am I! Send me."

Randy Bunch

New Life Church

Paso Robles, California

Chapter 1

WHAT WE OWE TO THE WORLD

I am a debtor both to Greeks and to barbarians, both to wise and to unwise. So, as much as is in me, I am ready to preach the gospel to you who are in Rome also. For I am not ashamed of the gospel of Christ, for it is the power of God to salvation for everyone who believes, for the Jew first and also for the Greek. (Romans 1:14-16)

Jesus said, "When someone has been given much, much will be required in return" (Luke 12:48, *NLT*). The Apostle Paul understood this. He had called himself "the chief of sinners" in his first epistle to Timothy, and understood all too well what it was to be forgiven.

Paul had been the greatest thorn in the early Church's side for some time – the point man in the persecution levied against the faithful of God. That is, until his dramatic conversion on the road to Damascus. In one amazing moment of mercy, Saul of Tarsus experienced the grace of forgiveness and became a new man; the man who would become the single greatest force for Christianity, next to Jesus, in the history of the Church.

His heart was changed and his malevolent designs against the Church forgotten. In the days that followed, he would receive a commission by the Head of the Church to take the Gospel he once persecuted to his own countrymen, the Gentiles, and even to the highest seats of power in the known world at that time. That commission would claim the rest of his life, and ultimately, he would end his life a martyr to the very cause he once sought to destroy.

Years later, Paul detailed this commission as he stood before King Agrippa, in chains.

Indeed, I myself thought I must do many things contrary to the name of Jesus of Nazareth. This I also did in Jerusalem, and many of the saints I shut up in prison, having received authority from the chief priests; and when they were put to death, I cast my vote against them. And I punished them often in every synagogue and compelled them to blaspheme; and being exceedingly enraged against them, I persecuted them even to foreign cities.

While thus occupied, as I journeyed to Damascus with authority and commission from the chief priests, at midday, O king, along the road I saw a light from heaven, brighter than the sun, shining around me and those who journeyed with me. And when we all had fallen to the ground, I heard a voice speaking to me and saying in the Hebrew language, "Saul, Saul, why are you persecuting Me? It is hard for you to kick against the goads." So I said, "Who are You, Lord?" And He said, "I am Jesus, whom you are persecuting. But rise and stand on your feet; for I have appeared to you for this purpose, to make you a minister and a witness both of the things which you have seen and of the things which I will yet reveal to you. I will deliver you from the Jewish people, as well as from the Gentiles, to whom I now send you, to open their eyes, in order to turn them from darkness to light, and from the power of Satan to God, that they may receive forgiveness of sins and an inheritance among those who are sanctified by faith in Me."

Therefore, King Agrippa, I was not disobedient to the heavenly vision, but declared first to those in Damascus and in Jerusalem, and throughout all the region of Judea, and then to the Gentiles, that they should repent, turn to God, and do works befitting repentance. (Acts 26:9-20)

In examining the life of the Apostle Paul and the many things he suffered for the sake of the Gospel, it is obvious how impactful his own experience of conversion was, and how it motivated him to fulfill the call on his life. He carried inside something that I believe is, to some degree, missing from the Church today; a sense of *indebtedness*.

Paul realized that what had happened for him on that road to Damascus was too good not to share with absolutely everyone else in the entire world. It's easy to see, as one reads the story of his life, that he was absolutely consumed, almost recklessly abandoned, to sharing the Gospel with every person he could, in every venue possible, all the time.

Without being accusatory or attempting to indict the Church for being apathetic as it concerns the lost, I think we would all admit that it is very easy in our modern culture, to put our obligation, our debt of winning the lost with the good news of Jesus Christ, behind a long list of other, less important priorities.

Paul said, "I am a debtor." This was not some debt he paid because of guilt he felt before God or pressure from people. This sense of indebtedness sprung from his awareness of what he had himself received in the form of God's grace and mercy. Paul was a debtor in the same way that a doctor who might find the cure for cancer would be a debtor to the many who are afflicted with that horrible disease. There are some things just too important *not* to share.

But there was something else Paul possessed along with his sense of indebtedness that made him a tireless and effective soul winner. That other trait was an absolute *confidence* in the power of the Gospel to change lives. Paul's repeated sharing of his own testimony is offered like evidence in a trial of the efficacy of the Gospel. It was this personal encounter with the Gospel's saving power that gave him the confidence to write, "For I am not ashamed of the gospel of Christ, *for it is the power of God unto salvation* for everyone who believes…" (Romans 1:16).

We all know that the best salesman is the one who is *sold* on his product. For many of us, our conscience would prohibit us from trying to push off on others something we didn't absolutely believe in ourselves. When I think of the confidence Paul had in his "product," it makes me think of a humorous story from my own past.

I had always said that I was *not* a salesman. I found the stereotypical image of the phony, fast-talking used car salesman just as obnoxious as most people do. I equated all salesmen with that kind of falseness and considered any qualities of salesmanship outside of my interest or skill set. That is, until I found a product I believed in!

Without telling you the name of the product (to save myself from a possible lawsuit), it was a diet pill, suspiciously billed as a "nutritional supplement." This product came out at the same time that many other "lose-weight-quick-without-diet-or-exercise" products were hitting the market. It would later be banned by the FDA, but while it was out there, it worked!

I was pastor of a church at the time, and one of my parishioners was taking this "magic" pill to help him shed the unwanted pounds around his middle. Inspired by his results, I bought some of the pills from his multi-level marketing matrix and headed down the path of quick results. Even before I lost the thirty-five pounds in three months (the height of my success with the product), I became a passionate advocate of this quick-fix pill and extolled its virtues to everyone with whom I came into contact. Both my excitement and my results were obvious, making me a compelling salesman!

I'm sorry to say that many others, inspired by my testimony and the obvious success I was having, also bought the pill to help them lose their unwanted weight. Now, many years older and a little wiser, I am embarrassed that I got caught up in what was obviously a very short-term solution to a problem that requires a little more discipline and little less "magic." Nevertheless, it served to show me the real qualities of a convincing salesman: real conviction from personal experience, and; the knowledge that others can be positively affected if they "buy in" to the product.

Like Paul, we are debtors, and the product we have to "sell" works for all people of all races all over the world, if only they will believe. They must "buy in" wholeheartedly, and it is we, the

Church, who are assigned the task of persuading, with all conviction, anyone who will listen.

To do this, we must also *know* our product. No salesman can be sure of himself if he isn't familiar with what he's supposed to be selling to others. While some may find the analogy of a salesman offensive when speaking of the Gospel, many of the same principles apply. In my opinion, the best salesmen are well-informed, sincere, and obviously believe that what they're representing is genuinely good for others. No one wants a salesman who is indifferent about his product or the customer, or who is there solely out of obligation because it's his job to sell. Such an attitude is no more appealing in a witness for Christ than it is in a salesman.

A good salesman finds a point of connection; a common interest or a shared background. This immediately causes the customer to drop his defenses as he is able to identify with the salesman on a more personal level. *He is not that different from me,* they might think, or *He seems like a good guy, like a lot of people I know back home. If he says it's a good product, it probably is.*

Paul understood this and endeavored in every way he could to identify with those to whom he ministered.

Even though I am free of the demands and expectations of everyone, I have voluntarily become a servant to any and all in order to reach a wide range of people: religious, nonreligious, meticulous moralists, loose-living immoralists, the defeated, the demoralized — whoever. I didn't take on their way of life. I kept my bearings in Christ — but I entered their world and tried to experience things from their point of view. I've become just about every sort of servant there is in my attempts to lead those I meet into a God-saved life. I did all this because of the Message. I didn't just want to talk about it; I wanted to be in on it! (1 Corinthians 9:19-23, MSG)

Like Paul, we should all want to be "in on it" too. Nothing could be more exciting, or more rewarding than seeing a life forever changed by the power of God because *you* stepped out and trusted Him to use your obedience to the Great Commission (see Matthew 28:18-20).

We might do many good things for others, but nothing could compare to the eternal good we might do through sharing our faith. Eternity alone will tell the story of what the seeds you planted in the hearts of others produced.

Chapter 2

HAVING A HEART TO HEAR

Then the brethren immediately sent Paul and Silas away by night to Berea. When they arrived, they went into the synagogue of the Jews. These were more fair-minded than those in Thessalonica, in that they received the word with all readiness, and searched the Scriptures daily to find out whether these things were so. (Acts 17:10-11)

For some, our study of the Gospel's saving power will redefine some terms, or at the very least, broaden them. So before we get too far into this study, I want to raise a caution flag and encourage you to approach this book with an open mind, just as you would any information that might challenge your already established convictions.

Sometimes, it's easy for those of us who have been raised under a particular biblical persuasion (or a religion other than Christianity) to feel disloyal at even entertaining another perspective, or listening with an open mind to the opinions of others. Yet we must be aware that the spiritual and cultural context in which we were raised creates a filter through which we see and hear everything. This can keep us from learning from others who have discovered truths still unknown to us.

Sometimes, discovering the truth means setting aside preconceived ideas and long, strongly held biases to gain a fresh perspective. It doesn't mean we're to abandon all we've ever been taught or believed, but we have to realize that none of us has all the truth.

Even the Apostle Paul said, "For we know *in part...*" (1 Corinthians 13:9). If Paul only knew *in part*, and he wrote the majority of the letters written to the Church in the New Testament, it's fair to say that the rest of us probably know a lot *smaller* part! If any of us believe that we, or our particular group have exclusive possession of all truth, we are deluded.

And if anyone thinks that he knows anything, he knows nothing yet as he ought to know. (1 Corinthians 8:2)

All of us are in process. In fact, the more we learn and mature, the more we see how truly little we know. It's a well-known fact that if you want to find someone who knows everything, just ask a first-year Bible school student – or better yet, your teenager!

It has been rightly said, "What we *think* we know is a far greater impediment to further growth and development than what we *don't* know." The reason for this is simple. When we *know* we are ignorant, or at least humble enough to realize that we don't have all the answers, we are wide open to hear and to receive new light and truth. However, when we think we already have the answers, we tend to shut ourselves off from further light and "circle the wagons" around our particular dogma, regardless of how it stands up to scriptural scrutiny.

For those of us who are already believers in Jesus Christ, we need to realize that we have a teacher on the inside of us who constantly endeavors to "lead and guide us into all truth" (John 16:13). If we will listen and stay open, the Holy Spirit will gently nudge us in the right direction.

> But the anointing which you have received from Him abides in you, and you do not need that anyone teach you; but as the same anointing teaches you concerning all things, and is true, and is not a lie, and just as it has taught you, you will abide in Him. (1 John 2:27)

This verse is not implying that we don't need teachers to instruct us in the truths of the Word of God. It is clear that God calls and anoints teachers and sets them in the Church to help equip us (see Ephesians 4:11-12). But this verse *is* saying that we have an indwelling teacher who will lead and guide us into truth so that we might experience all that God has for us. We can *trust* that inward compass because it is the very Spirit of Truth who is witnessing to our hearts and leading us accordingly.

This was true for me years ago when I found myself hungry for more of God. Notice that word, *hungry*. In my experience, there is little that can substitute for hunger. God "satisfies the *longing* soul, and fills the *hungry* soul with goodness" (Psalm 107:9). Hunger keeps us moving forward in God and keeps us open to fresh insights from the Holy Spirit. Hungry people are humble people. Hungry people are spiritually healthy people as well. The smug, self-satisfied believer who thinks he has cornered the market on truth ceases to grow, and his spiritual life stagnates and sours.

At this time, I had hit a plateau in my walk with God, and I was frustrated. My heart kept telling me there was more, and God had placed people in my life who shared with me their experiences of being filled with the Holy Spirit. The problem was that my particular denomination vehemently disagreed with the charismatic experience of being filled with the Holy Spirit, and speaking with other tongues. Speaking with tongues in particular seemed to illicit the most dramatic, even hostile objections.

Most of what I heard about speaking with other tongues, however, had more to do with subjective experiences or emotional reactions than the hard evidence of Scripture. It wouldn't be, in fact, until after I had received this experience that I really gained a firm, scriptural foundation on the subject. Indeed, later on, I had the opportunity to go back into some of the very Pentecostal and Charismatic churches that had helped me and teach *them* on the subject.

Had someone been able to sit down and take time with me, showing me the scriptural grounds for the experience in the Word, I think I would have received the Baptism in the Holy Spirit much sooner. I have said over the years that I would have been filled with the Holy Spirit much sooner had it not been for Pentecostals!

The truth is that when I finally did receive the experience, it was as though I was dragged in by my heart, my head kicking and screaming all the way. On an intellectual level, I probably could have argued more convincingly *against* the experience than *for* it. That's not to say I hadn't begun to see the truth of it in the Word. God had begun to lead me to the passages in the New Testament that I needed to see for my heart to open up. But the fact is, I received the Baptism in the Holy Spirit because I was so hungry for God that my heart was willing to set aside its prejudices and preconceived notions to receive more from Him.

On April 1, 1984 (yes, April Fool's Day), I prayed a simple prayer that proceeded forth from a heart starving for God, one that had begun to see only the smallest bit of scriptural light shining in from under the door, as it were. I prayed, "God, if there is more of you to be had, I want it!" I had heard one of my spiritual fathers in the faith say that he had seen many people receive this experience from God through just such a prayer. But for me, it was just the honest cry of my heart to have all God had for me.

Having said all this, I am *not* advocating for you to abandon your convictions and embrace any doctrine or experience on scripturally flimsy evidence. At the same time, however, I would not have you shut your heart off when the Holy Spirit is clearly trying to nudge you into a deeper experience, even when it seems to fly in the face of what you've been taught previously. The fact is, we don't know that much, and God is ever shedding more light in our hearts, leading us into deeper places in our walk with Him.

For me, this awakening to truth came over time, as I studied the Word and the Holy Spirit dealt with my very stubborn heart. I remember Him asking me, "Randy, are you perfect?" (The question was in regard to what I *thought* I knew.) No, it wasn't a voice or a question like one man might ask another. Rather, it was God dealing with my heart; the Spirit challenging my assumptions of what I believed to be truth. He was asking me to examine why I believed what I believed.

I remember Him challenging me on why I thought my particular denomination was right about certain Bible subjects rather than the other group down the street that clearly loved Him as much as we did. The ultimate discovery for me, and what I should have seen without so much difficulty, was that I believed what I believed because someone I trusted – a pastor, parent, or Sunday-School teacher – told me it was true.

As well-intentioned as those people were, I began to realize that when the devil came around to challenge my faith, it would not be enough for me to say, "Well, this is what I was *told* the Bible said." I couldn't make him flee saying, "It is written in the material that comes from my denomination!" I had to know the Word for myself. The Bible gives us the perfect, balanced approach with which to pursue our search for truth, whether it be in the form of a sermon on Sunday morning, a friend sharing his or her ideas, or whatever. Notice the verse we quoted at the beginning of this chapter:

> These (the people of Berea) were more fair-minded than those in Thessalonica, in that they received the word with all readiness, and searched the Scriptures daily to find out whether these things were so. (Acts 17:11)

These Bereans were hungry for truth and had an eager ear to hear all that Paul and Silas said. Nevertheless, they weren't gullible enough to just swallow everything they heard, either. They checked all they heard against the Word of God to verify its truthfulness. In my experience, that combination is very rare. I have met people who were argumentative and always wanted to debate, and others who were like baby birds with eyes shut and mouths open, ready to swallow whatever anyone poked down their spiritual throat. It is truly wonderful to see someone who possesses a hungry, open heart, and yet has the good sense to listen to his or her own spirit and do the homework.

That is how I am encouraging you to approach this teaching on the Gospel's saving power. For some, it may be nothing new, and may only serve to remind them of what they know. There's nothing wrong with that! We need to continuously feed on the Word to keep our faith strong. But for some, this book may pose a conflict, challenging them to accept new ideas and broaden their perspective. I can only encourage you to be a good "Berean": study with an open heart and follow along closely to make sure that what I've written is backed up with the Word of God. Do your own study, searching the Scriptures whenever you need assurance that there is a biblical foundation for what is being taught. Such habits will serve you well.

Remember, Solomon said, "He who answers a matter before he hears it, it is folly and shame to him" (Proverbs 18:13). I like the *New Living Translation* that puts it this way, "Spouting off before listening to the facts is both shameful and foolish."

By no means do I claim that this small book is the definitive word on this subject. It is an admittedly brief and partial covering of the subject. But you are not limited by what I, or any other human teacher, writes or says. The Holy Spirit can take the truths presented in this little book and open a world of truth to you that can set you on a new course of discovery. And now, having set the stage, let's look at what the Bible has to say about what it means to be *saved*.

Chapter 3

UNDERSTANDING OUR COMPREHENSIVE SALVATION

For I am not ashamed of the gospel of Christ, *for it is the power of God to salvation* for everyone who believes, for the Jew first and also for the Greek. (Romans 1:16)

As we begin our study on the Gospel's saving power, it is essential that we begin by defining some terms. Paul declared the gospel to be the *power* of God. Often, when we think of the power of God we think back to the miracles of Moses: the splitting of the Red Sea, or the ten plagues of Egypt, which brought to its knees the mightiest empire in the world at that time. We might think of Joshua commanding the sun to stand still in the sky so he could accomplish a great military victory for Israel, or Jesus feeding the multitudes, healing the sick, or even raising the dead.

Certainly, those are demonstrations of the power of God, but Paul says that God's power to save is in the *Gospel*. The New Testament was originally written in the Greek language, and the word for "power" in Romans 1:16 is the Greek word *dunamis*. From one form of this Greek word we get our word, *dynamite*. It literally means *force, power, ability*, or *might*. It further implies the idea of *inherent power*, or power that resides in a thing by virtue of its nature. In other words, the Gospel has power, force, ability and might inherently within itself. For what purpose? To *save!*

Paul, under the inspiration of the Holy Spirit, said that the Gospel of Jesus Christ is the "power of God unto *salvation*." But here again, we must define our terms. Due to our varying backgrounds, we bring to the table different ideas of what the word *salvation* means.

In the church in which I was raised, when we said someone got *saved* or received *salvation*, we meant one thing and one thing only – they got *born again!* They asked Jesus into their heart to be their Lord and Savior, and received eternal life.

We will go into what it really means to be *born again* in a later chapter, but for now, the point is, we understood salvation to mean *spiritual* salvation and pretty much nothing else. We weren't wrong, but we weren't completely right either. Yes, the word, "salvation," encompasses spiritual salvation and the new birth, but its meaning is much broader than that.

The word, "salvation," in Romans 1:16 is translated from the Greek word, *soteria*. The verb form of the word, "saved," is the Greek word *sozo* and means essentially the same thing. *Soteria* means *deliverance, preservation, safety*, and of course, *salvation*. Perhaps one of the most helpful definitions of this word, however, comes from C.I. Scofield, the author of the *Scofield Reference Edition Bible*. In his commentary on Romans 1:16, Dr. Scofield said the following:

> The Hebrew and Greek words for "salvation" imply the ideas of deliverance, safety, preservation, healing and soundness: "Salvation" is the great inclusive word of the gospel, gathering into itself all the redemptive acts and processes: as justification, redemption, grace, propitiation, imputation, forgiveness, sanctification and glorification...[1]

In other words, this word, *soteria,* does not mean just spiritual salvation or receiving eternal life, but encompasses all the benefits and privileges of the redemption God purchased for us through Jesus Christ. When Christ redeemed us, He purchased for us a *full* salvation that encompasses every aspect of our lives.

> He who did not spare His own Son, but delivered Him up for us all, *how shall He not with Him also freely give us all things?* (Romans 8:32)

I do not for one moment want you to think we are trying to downplay the importance of the forgiveness of sin and our deliverance from its *spiritual* consequences. It is, in fact, because Jesus dealt with our sin on the cross that we can enjoy all the blessings of God. But neither do I want you to limit yourself from enjoying *all* that Christ purchased for you through a failure to understand the comprehensive nature of your salvation. After all, the blessings Christ secured for us came at the ultimate price.

You prepare a table before me in the presence of my enemies… (Psalm 23:5)

As we'll see, that banqueting table of redemption has blessings on it that cover every need we have in life. Many have erroneously thought that this "table" refers to the blessings on God's *heavenly* banqueting table; blessings relegated to "the sweet by and by." But this cannot be the case, for this is a banqueting table we enjoy "in the presence of our enemies." There are no enemies in Heaven! The enemies we face are down here, and we contend with them right now, in this life on earth.

Some would have us believe that God has made provision for us *spiritually*, but when it comes to natural, physical, or material needs, we're more or less on our own. Some have even gone so far as to imply that suffering lack, sickness, and tragedy bring us closer to God. If that were the case, we should all be praying for God to make us sick and broke, and for tragedy to strike us at every turn. Nothing could be more foolish, and I don't believe anyone truly *believes* that.

To say that God brings destruction and calamity into our lives to perfect us *spiritually* is to say that God does things to His children for which we would put a natural father in jail. This does not line up with a God who is love (1 John 4:8), who is good (Psalm 145:8-9) and who gives good things (James 1:17), especially to His children. In fact, the Scriptures are clear that we can see something of the Father nature of God in the way we care for our own children.

If you then, being evil, know how to give good gifts to your children, how much more will your Father who is in heaven give good things to those who ask Him! (Matthew 7:11)

The most hardened of men can be changed when a child comes into their lives. They will go to great lengths to secure the physical and financial welfare of their children. They might make great sacrifices to see to it that their children have the advantages they never enjoyed. But no natural father can claim to have made the sacrifices for his children that our Heavenly Father made for us, for it was through the sacrifice of Jesus, His only begotten Son, that God secured this comprehensive salvation.

It's true that because of sin there is suffering in the earth. But we have confused the consequences of man's rebellion with God's will. If you want to see what God's will for man is, you need to look back to the Garden of Eden, before the fall, where His good intentions for man were first revealed, and to the cross where He showed the lengths to which He would go to restore man to his lost inheritance. Jesus' arms were not just stretched across the wooden beam into which His hands were nailed; they were spread out to embrace all of fallen humanity in the single greatest demonstration of selfless love this universe will ever witness.

It was through the redemption He purchased for us on that cross that our salvation came; a salvation that includes forgiveness and healing, soundness and safety, peace and prosperity, and ultimately, restoration to God's original purpose for us. I say to those wanting to postpone our Psalm 23:5 feast until we get to Heaven, "How dare we allow the blessings of God to rot on the banquet table of redemption when they came at such an extraordinary cost!"

My friend, we can feast in the face of our foes right here in this life! God has made complete provision for us, *naturally* as well as *spiritually*, and for our all our needs, both *temporal* and *eternal!* Notice what Peter says about this in his second epistle.

Grace and peace be multiplied to you in the knowledge of God and of Jesus our Lord, as His divine power has given to us all things that pertain to life and godliness, through the knowledge of Him who called us by glory and virtue, by which have been given to us exceedingly great and precious promises, that through these you may be partakers of the divine nature, having escaped the corruption that is in the world through lust. (2 Peter 1:2-4)

Notice that Peter says, "(God's) divine power has given us all things that pertain to *life* (natural needs) and *godliness* (spiritual needs)." That *power* is inherent in the Gospel, as we've already seen from Romans 1:16. It's there, in the Gospel, that we can gain the knowledge of God by which "grace and peace (might) be multiplied" to us.

As we believe and exercise faith in the Gospel of Jesus Christ, God's power is released on our behalf to meet every need we'll ever face in this life and, at the same time, prepare us for the life to come! It's through those "exceeding great and precious promises" that we become "partakers of the divine nature."

When I think of the comprehensive salvation God provided for us, I cannot help but think of a humorous story from my days in traveling ministry. For a number of years, I traveled across the country with another minister, Rick Ramsey, conducting what we (and others at the time) called *Holy Ghost Meetings*. They were wonderful times of allowing the Holy Spirit to both inspire us in the ministry of the Word and also to demonstrate His presence and power through the gifts of the Spirit.

It seemed as if the Church was in a wonderful *season of the supernatural* during this time, the mid-nineties. Ministers who had never before dared to wander from the security of their notes were finding a new level of inspiration in their preaching. The glory and joy of the Lord were often demonstrated in church services. We rode this wave with many others who recognized the move of the Spirit, and we saw God do wonderful things, setting people free as He moved powerfully among them. Just the stories alone from those years would make a wonderful book in itself.

On one particular night, we were in Big Bear, California. In those days, we were very open to the Holy Spirit in regard to the direction we would take in the services. Sometimes, Rick would start the service and I would follow later, and sometimes I would begin and he would follow me. It just depended on how, and upon whom, the Lord was moving. In this particular service, I began and preached on the benefits of God from Psalm 103.

> Bless the Lord, O my soul;
> And all that is within me, bless His holy name!
> Bless the Lord, O my soul,
> And forget not all His benefits:
> Who forgives all your iniquities,
> Who heals all your diseases,
> Who redeems your life from destruction,
> Who crowns you with lovingkindness and tender mercies,
> Who satisfies your mouth with good things,
> So that your youth is renewed like the eagle's.
> (Psalm 103:1-5)

By gifting, both Rick and I are teachers, but very often in this season of ministry, the Lord would put a pretty good preaching anointing on us. This was definitely one of those nights. I was preaching strong and hard on the benefits of God. In fact, I had such a good head of steam that night I thought I might just take the whole service.

Suddenly, right in the middle of my message, I felt the anointing of the Spirit lift from me. I knew immediately what was happening. This always occurred when the Spirit of God had quickened something to the other guy. When that anointing lifted from the one speaking, it was time to defer to the one sitting by, as God had given him what was to follow. This operation of the Spirit, seen too little in the Church today, is in the Word of God.

Let two or three prophets speak, and let the others judge. *But if anything is revealed to another who sits by, let the first keep silent.* For you can all prophesy one by one, that all may learn and all may be encouraged. (1 Corinthians 14:29-31)

Whenever that anointing lifted off one of us, we knew the other was ready to go. We became so proficient flowing together in this way that often the exchange was seamless, and it provided a unique demonstration of spiritual ministry that was a lesson in itself. Sometimes, while we were ministering the Word, the Spirit would use us together in the gifts of the Spirit, such as tongues and interpretation, or one might even demonstrate what the other was teaching.

When I felt that anointing lift, I immediately found a quick stopping place and looked to Rick, ready to head to my seat to enjoy whatever God had placed in his spirit to share. Strangely, however,

Rick looked hesitant and waved me off. This was surprising, as we usually never missed a step. On this occasion, however, Rick was stalling. I would have gone on if I could have, but once the anointing lifts off of you you're done! (This is something every minister would do well to learn!)

I prevailed on Rick again, probably saying something like, "Go ahead, come on up and give what you've got." Finally, knowing he just had to step out and obey God, Rick stepped up to the pulpit. As soon as he began, I knew why he had been reluctant. "Well," he said, "There was this guy who owned a dog...," and he went on to tell a joke; one I later found out he had first read in *Reader's Digest!*

The joke was about a guy who had a bird dog he wanted trained. After the dog spent a couple weeks with the trainer, the owner accompanied the trainer and his dog to a large open field with lots of trees for a demonstration of what his dog had learned.

At a command from the trainer, the dog headed quickly to a smaller tree in the field. At the base of the tree, the dog stopped and, standing in place, turned two full circles. The trainer turned to the owner of the dog and said, "See that tree? There are two birds in it." The trainer grabbed a rock, threw it at the tree and, sure enough, two birds flew out.

The owner was happy with the result, and the trainer proceeded with the demonstration. This time, he pointed to a larger tree. On stopping at the foot of the tree, the dog circled five times. Sure enough, five birds flew out of the tree after the trainer threw the rock. He repeated this a few times. Each time, the number of the dog's circles equaled the number of birds in the tree.

Finally, the trainer took them to the back of the field to a huge tree. He pointed and once again the dog took off toward the tree, just as before. However, this time, instead of turning around to indicate how many birds were in the tree, the dog looked quickly around him, picked up a stick in its jaws and began shaking it vigorously. The trainer turned to the owner and said, "See that tree? There are more birds in that tree than you can shake a stick at!"

Our audience at the church in Big Bear began to laugh, both at the story and at the unusual turn the service had taken. Then Rick said, "God wants you to know that He has more benefits than you can shake a stick at!" At that point, the Spirit fell. What a service we had!

The point was powerfully made: we can try to enumerate all the benefits of God, and even describe the comprehensive nature of salvation, but in the end, God simply has more benefits than you can shake a stick at!

Blessed be the God and Father of our Lord Jesus Christ, who has blessed us with *every spiritual blessing* in the heavenly places in Christ. (Ephesians 1:3)

Chapter 4

SALVATION IN THE NAME

The Bible is God's self-revelation to man. Jesus, who is the ultimate revelation of God (see Hebrews 1:3), is found on every page of both the Old and New Testaments.

After His resurrection, Jesus appeared to two of His downcast disciples as they walked on the road to Emmaus, a village just outside of Jerusalem. Their hopes, they thought, had been crushed by the murder of their Messiah at the hands of Jewish leaders and the Roman government. As the two broken-hearted disciples talked with each other about these things, Jesus, keeping His identity hidden from them, came alongside and asked what they were discussing between themselves.

After giving Him an account of the events surrounding His own death and burial, they expressed their disillusionment. They also expressed their confusion regarding the reports of His resurrection from the women who had seen the angels at the tomb after He had risen.

Finally, Jesus breaks in and reprimands them for their unbelief and failure to see the overarching plan of God in the events that had occurred.

> Then He said to them, "O foolish ones, and slow of heart to believe in all that the prophets have spoken! Ought not the Christ to have suffered these things and to enter into His glory?" *And beginning at Moses and all the Prophets, He expounded to them in all the Scriptures the things concerning Himself.* (Luke 24:25-27)

As they walked together on that road, Jesus gave the two disciples a personal, one-on-two Bible study about Himself, His life, and His purpose. He had plenty of material since He was able to draw from the entire text of the Old Testament. He is revealed in every type, from the sacrifices to the articles in the temple, and from the brazen serpent in the wilderness to the Passover lamb.

God has not left us without witness of Himself. In the whole of the Word, we have an ever increasing self-revelation from God Himself of who He is and what He is like. In fact, His very names are a revelation to us of who He is. In the Bible account of the burning bush, where God calls Moses to deliver the children of Israel out of Egyptian bondage, He touches on this truth.

> I appeared to Abraham, to Isaac, and to Jacob, as God Almighty, but by My name Lord I was not known to them. (Exodus 6:3)

We can see that God's revelation of Himself is progressive. The patriarchs saw something of who God is, but now, to Moses and his generation, He is going to further reveal something of Himself. What we read as "God Almighty" in our English Bibles is actually the proper name, *El Shaddai*. This name speaks to the power of God, as our English translation suggests. It does indeed mean "God Almighty" and reveals Him as the "all sufficient one." There is no impossibility with El Shaddai; no need He cannot meet, no problem He cannot solve, and no promise He will not keep. El Shaddai speaks to the ability of God. El Shaddai is the God who *can*.

However, there is a further revelation of God that is to be found in the name we have translated as "Lord" in our English Bible. It is the Hebrew name, *Jehovah*, or *Yaweh*. Jehovah is the *redemptive* name of God and speaks to His disposition toward us; His desire to bless us and deliver us. While El Shaddai reveals Him as the God who *can*, Jehovah reveals Him as the God who *will!*

We will now examine seven compound, covenant-keeping names of God (Jehovah titles), each of which reveals a different aspect of His redemptive disposition toward us. Since Jehovah is God's *redemptive* name, the benefits revealed in God's Jehovah titles foreshadow blessings we have now through the finished work of Christ, and show the comprehensive nature of the salvation God provided for us through Him.

These Jehovah names are, in no particular order:

Jehovah-Shammah, "The Lord is Present," or "The Lord is There" (Ezekiel 48:35).

Again, what we read in Ezekiel 48:35 as "The Lord is There" is actually a proper name in the Hebrew language of the Old Testament. The same holds true with each of these names.

Jehovah-Shalom, "The Lord our Peace" (Judges 6:24)

Jehovah-Ra-ah, "The Lord our Shepherd" (Psalm 23:1)

Jehovah-Nissi, "The Lord our Banner" or "Victory" (Exodus 17:15)

Jehovah-Tsidkenu, "The Lord our Righteousness" (Jeremiah 23:6)

Jehovah-Jireh, "The Lord our Provider" (Genesis 22:14)

Jehovah-Rapha, "The Lord our Healer" (Exodus 15:26)

These seven names reveal a comprehensive provision, or *salvation*. Through Him we have the assurance of His presence, of peace, of guidance and protection, of victory, of right standing with God, of provision for any and every need, and healing for our bodies. Again, these were benefits enjoyed by God's people in the Old Testament, but all such blessings and benefits shown to mankind have but one source.

It's important to realize that due to man's sin, the only thing we could justly receive from the hand of God was judgment. All the blessings and mercy shown to the children of Israel in the Old Testament were given on the basis of a promissory note of the redemption God would purchase for us at Calvary. To put it another way, God blessed them on credit – credit that would be paid at the cross. It was there that the price for sin was paid, and the scales of divine justice were balanced, once for all.

That's why these names reveal the comprehensive *salvation* we have through Christ. Had Jesus not paid the price for our sins, we would be eternally lost and hopeless; condemned to a future of eternal torment. But thank God, He paid that price fully for you and me!

And He [that same Jesus Himself] is the propitiation (the atoning sacrifice) for our sins, and not for ours alone but also for [the sins of] the whole world. (1 John 2:2, AMP)

He didn't just save us *from* the consequences of our sin, but *into* an inheritance in which our every need is gloriously met.

Giving thanks to the Father *who has qualified* us to be partakers of the inheritance of the saints in the light. *He has delivered us from the power of darkness and conveyed us into the kingdom of the Son of His love.* (Colossians 1:12-13)

It's through Jesus that we can know God in all His saving grace and glory. In fact, it's *His* name that comprehends all the benefits of God revealed in these Old Testament names. The name "Jesus" means *Savior.*

And she will bring forth a Son, and you shall call His name Jesus, for He will save His people from their sins. (Matthew 1:21)

Through Jesus, we know God's wondrous love and provision. His benevolent, redemptive disposition toward us was revealed in that decisive moment in history when Jesus took upon Himself the guilt of the human race and became the object of God's divine wrath so that judgment might pass over you and me, and mercy and grace would be given to us instead.

So now, to the one who is feeling abandoned in the time of crisis, He is Jehovah-Shammah, "The Lord is There" or "The Lord is Present."

And I will pray the Father, and He will give you another Helper, *that He may abide with you forever.* (John 14:16)

None of us ever need to feel alone or abandoned during times of crisis or difficulty. His abiding, comforting, and *saving* presence is there to see us through the darkest valleys of life. As the psalmist said, "Even when I walk through the darkest valley, I will not be afraid, for you are close beside me" (Psalm 23:4, NLT).

To the one feeling inner turmoil who can find no rest, He is Jehovah-Shalom, "The Lord our Peace."

Peace I leave with you, My peace I give to you; not as the world gives do I give to you. Let not your heart be troubled, neither let it be afraid. (John 14:27)

Consider the immense fortune an entrepreneur would amass if he could "bottle" peace and put it on the market. It's the one thing money *cannot* buy and the one thing that all the world wants. People medicate themselves with prescription drugs and drown themselves in every sensual pleasure to forget the things that their hearts cannot escape. Yet, to the believer who walks in his inheritance, peace is his portion.

To the one needing guidance and direction in life, He is Jehovah-Ra-ah, "The Lord our Shepherd."

For as many as are led by the Spirit of God, these are sons of God. (Romans 8:14)

Jesus, our Shepherd, will never leave us to our own aimless wanderings. He has a plan and purpose for our lives and will direct our feet into His perfect path, causing us to "lie down in green pastures" as He leads us "beside the still waters." These images from Psalm 23 reveal both the provision and tranquility God wants us enjoy in *this* life!

To the one feeling overwhelmed and defeated by life's circumstances, He is Jehovah-Nissi, "The Lord our Victory."

> But thanks be to God, who gives us the victory through our Lord Jesus Christ. (1 Corinthians 15:57)

We don't fight our battles alone; in fact, they have already been fought and won through the salvation Jesus provided for us at Calvary. It was through the cross that provision was made to see us through every challenge this life has to offer. That doesn't mean we won't have trials or that we won't have to "fight the good fight of faith" (though thankfully that is a fight we can win). As Paul said, "Yet in all these things we are *more than conquerors* through Him who loved us" (Romans 8:37).

To the one who feels he can't even lift his eyes toward his God for shame, He is Jehovah-Tsidkenu, "The Lord our Righteousness."

> For He made Him who knew no sin to be sin for us, that we might become the righteousness of God in Him. (2 Corinthians 5:21)

The blood of Jesus, which was shed for the remission of our sins, has power to both legally cleanse us and "cleanse our conscience" (Hebrews 9:14) so that we might stand guiltless before God. Because of our High Priest, Jesus Christ, we can "come boldly to the throne of grace, that we may obtain mercy and find grace to help in time of need" (Hebrews 4:16).

To the one who cannot make ends meet for lack, He is Jehovah-Jireh, "The Lord our Provider."

> And my God shall supply all your need according to His riches in glory by Christ Jesus. (Philippians 4:19)

Our God is not only concerned that our spiritual needs are met, but our emotional and material needs as well. It was in the context of *money* that Paul, under the inspiration of the Spirit of God, wrote the above verse about meeting our every need. While we tend to think of our needs categorically, God saw the overall picture of our needs and, through the sacrifice of His Son, redeemed us completely, making provision for every area of life.

Lastly, to the one who is sick in body, He will show Himself as Jehovah-Rapha, "The Lord our Healer."

> Who Himself bore our sins in His own body on the tree,
> that we, having died to sins, might live for righteousness –
> by whose stripes you were healed. (1 Peter 2:24)

While we will devote much more space to this particular benefit in subsequent chapters, it is worth noting that this was the very first Jehovah title God revealed after the children of Israel were delivered from Egyptian bondage.

> So Moses brought Israel from the Red Sea; then they went
> out into the Wilderness of Shur. And they went three days
> in the wilderness and found no water. Now when they came

to Marah, they could not drink the waters of Marah, for they were bitter. Therefore the name of it was called Marah (Marah means bitter). And the people complained against Moses, saying, "What shall we drink?" So he cried out to the Lord, and the Lord showed him a tree. When he cast it into the waters, the waters were made sweet.

There He made a statute and an ordinance for them, and there He tested them, and said, "If you diligently heed the voice of the Lord your God and do what is right in His sight, give ear to His commandments and keep all His statutes, I will put none of the diseases on you which I have brought on the Egyptians. For I am the Lord who heals you (Jehovah-Rapha)." (Exodus 15:22-26)

Here we have as plain a type and picture of healing through the atonement as one could ever want. In light of this passage and others, it baffles me why some theologians try to say that healing was not provided for us in the atonement.

Most all will agree that the tree Moses cast into the bitter waters is a type or picture of the cross of Christ. It was through the application of this "tree" to their "bitter" situation that healing came to the waters. Furthermore, it was in the striking light of this picture of Calvary that God established His covenant to be their healer, even revealing Himself as Jehovah-Rapha, "the Lord who heals you."

It is ridiculous to imply that the children of Israel enjoyed the benefit of physical healing through a type or picture of Christ's redeeming work that we can't enjoy now, especially since that redemption has been fully accomplished. If the tree Moses cast into the bitter waters of Marah (a mere type of the cross) brought healing, how much more will the tree upon which Christ bore our sins bring healing to our bodies? (See 1 Peter 2:24.)

Not only does this imply physical healing, but I submit to you that no matter what the need, an application of the cross of Christ will make your bitter sweet! God can heal your finances, your marriage, your family, your broken heart, your backslidings (Jeremiah 3:22), and He will certainly heal your body! This is the comprehensive salvation He died to provide.

Too often we have sold God short in representing Him and His graciousness to the world. He did not pay the ultimate price for our salvation only to deny us the very blessings Christ died to provide. His answer to all our needs is, "Yes, I have an answer for that" (see 2 Corinthians 1:20). There is no need that you or anyone else will ever have that is not covered in the comprehensive salvation provided for us through Jesus.

For "whoever calls on the *name of the Lord* shall be *saved*." (Romans 10:13)

Chapter 5

THE CATALYST
OF FAITH

For I am not ashamed of the gospel of Christ, for it is the power of God to salvation *for everyone who believes,* for the Jew first and also for the Greek. (Romans 1:16)

So far, we've seen that the Gospel is the *power* of God unto salvation; that God's power is inherently in the Gospel to *save.* We've also seen that the word, *salvation,* is much broader in its meaning than many in the Church have realized. It includes deliverance, not only from the spiritual effects of man's sin, but from natural consequences of sin, such as poverty, sickness, and destruction as well. As we saw earlier, David saw this as he penned one of his famous psalms:

Bless the Lord, O my soul,
And forget not all His benefits:
Who forgives all your iniquities,

Who heals all your diseases,
Who redeems your life from destruction,
Who crowns you with lovingkindness and tender mercies,
Who satisfies your mouth with good things,
So that your youth is renewed like the eagle's.
(Psalm 103:2-5)

I remember hearing a theologian try to explain away healing as one of God's benefits, while commenting on this psalm. He said, "Well, I believe that God heals all our sicknesses, but He doesn't heal them all the time." But if you're going to say that about *healing*, you're going to have to go back to the line above that one and say, "He forgives us all our iniquities, but He doesn't forgive them all the time." David extols the goodness of God by declaring His faithfulness to heal as well as forgive. He tells us to rehearse the benefits of God, which include forgiveness of sin, healing for our bodies, and deliverance from destruction.

The fact is, God lifted mankind out of a horrible pit through the finished work of Jesus, who died for our sins and was raised again by the power of God, that He might justify all who believe in Him and give them an everlasting inheritance. This includes provision for every area of this life. God took man at his lowest and raised him to His highest.

But God, who is rich in mercy, because of His great love with which He loved us, even when we were dead in trespasses, made us alive together with Christ (by grace you have been saved), and raised us up together, and made us sit together in the heavenly places in Christ Jesus. (Ephesians 2:4-6)

Legally, the work has been done. The sacrifice has been offered and the scales of divine justice have been balanced. Judicially, all of mankind is released from the effects of Adam's sin. Look at how Paul speaks of our reconciliation to God through Jesus:

> Now all things are of God, *who has reconciled us to Himself through Jesus Christ,* and has given us the ministry of reconciliation, that is, that God was in Christ *reconciling the world to Himself, not imputing their trespasses to them,* and has committed to us the word of reconciliation. (2 Corinthians 5:18-19)

Notice in the verses above that God *has* reconciled us to Himself through Jesus Christ. He is no longer "imputing" our trespasses to us because Christ paid the price for our sin. Jesus' sacrifice reversed the evil Adam did when he rebelled against God's authority in the Garden, condemning man to everlasting judgment.

> But there is a great difference between Adam's sin and God's gracious gift. For the sin of this one man, Adam, brought death to many. But even greater is God's wonderful grace and his gift of forgiveness to many through this other man, Jesus Christ. And the result of God's gracious gift is very different from the result of that one man's sin. For Adam's sin led to condemnation, but God's free gift leads to our being made right with God, even though we are guilty of many sins. For the sin of this one man, Adam, caused death to rule over many. But even greater is God's wonderful grace and his gift of righteousness, for all who receive it will live in triumph over sin and death through this one man, Jesus Christ. (Romans 5:15-17, NLT)

Adam and Jesus stand as the two federal heads of the human race (see 1 Corinthians 15:21-22). In Adam, all are dead because of sin. But in Christ, all are made alive because of the sacrifice He made to pay the price for that sin. So, the question is, "Are you in Adam, or are you in Christ?"

All of us are *born* into Adam, our natural father, who passed onto us our fallen, sinful condition. Jesus came to undo what Adam did, making it possible for us to experience reconciliation with God. The work has been done, but for it to become a vital reality in *your* life, *you* have to believe that message of reconciliation and *respond* to the Gospel. Notice again that Romans 5:17 *(NLT)* says, "But even greater is God's wonderful grace and his gift of righteousness, *for all who receive it* will live in triumph over sin and death through this one man, Jesus Christ."

This is why the ministry of reconciliation is committed to the Church. If those still lost in their sins do not believe the Gospel and embrace it for themselves, they will spend an eternity lost and without hope, even though the price was completely paid for their salvation.

As I said, you were born into Adam. You have to be *born again* into Christ by identifying with Him as your substitute on Calvary's cross, believing that God raised Him from the dead to be the Savior of all who will call upon Him. Let's go back to Romans 1:16 and notice something vital.

> For I am not ashamed of the gospel of Christ, for it is the power of God to salvation *for everyone who believes*, for the Jew first and also for the Greek. (Romans 1:16)

Notice that the Gospel is *not* the power of God unto salvation for just anyone. There is a qualifier. The Gospel's saving power is released to those who *believe!* Faith is the *catalyst* which releases the Gospel's saving power into the life of the hearer.

God's power resides in the Gospel, ready to save, to heal, and deliver – to totally transform a life. But until that Word is mixed with faith by the hearer, God's power is not released. This is a most crucial and pivotal truth, for without this understanding, all is lost.

It is not enough to hear and merely entertain the truths of the Gospel. It is not enough to believe the Bible has merit and is a good guide for life and moral conduct. For the saving power of God to be released, one must personally believe and *mix his or her faith* with the Gospel. Notice the illustration given of the children of Israel.

> For indeed the gospel was preached to us as well as to them (speaking of the children of Israel); but the word which they heard *did not profit them*, not being *mixed with faith* in those who heard it. (Hebrews 4:2)

The writer of Hebrews is likening the promise God gave the children of Israel to the Gospel of Jesus Christ. Indeed, their "Gospel" was good news, especially after over four hundred years of slavery! He was giving them a Promised Land which flowed with milk and honey. This was a land that drank waters from the rain of heaven, a stark contrast to the dry and barren land of Egypt from which they came. This land would produce its crops and yield its bounty to them so that their days would be like days of heaven upon the earth (see Deuteronomy 11:6-21). That sounds pretty good, doesn't it? That's why it's called *good news!*

However, despite God's assurance that the land was theirs, the entire generation that came out of Egypt with Moses died in the wilderness and did not inherit the land God promised them. Why? Was God not true to His promise? Of course He was. He gave them the land. It was theirs by promise, but *they* failed to inherit it because of their unbelief.

The Old Testament book of Numbers records the sad story of how the children of Israel refused to go in and take the land God had given them. Their fear of the giants who inhabited the land, and the walled cities which stood in their way, talked them out of their faith just as they were poised to go in and possess the land. The men whom Moses sent in to spy out the land returned after forty days with evidence of the land's fruitfulness, but also a fear-filled account of what they had seen.

> Now they departed and came back to Moses and Aaron and all the congregation of the children of Israel in the Wilderness of Paran, at Kadesh; they brought back word to them and to all the congregation, and showed them the fruit of the land. Then they told him, and said: "We went to the land where you sent us. It truly flows with milk and honey, and this is its fruit. Nevertheless the people who dwell in the land are strong; the cities are fortified and very large; moreover we saw the descendants of Anak there. The Amalekites dwell in the land of the South; the Hittites, the Jebusites, and the Amorites dwell in the mountains; and the Canaanites dwell by the sea and along the banks of the Jordan." (Numbers 13:26-29)

At this point, Caleb, one of the spies whom Moses had sent, tried to calm the congregation's growing panic, assuring them of God's faithfulness and their ability to take possession of what He had promised them.

> Then Caleb quieted the people before Moses, and said, "Let us go up at once and take possession, for we are well able to overcome it." (Numbers 13:30)

Caleb's faith was based not on what he had seen in the land, but on the promise of God. He had seen the same cities and the same giants but chose to place his confidence in the good news of God's promise. Because of his faith, Caleb said, "We can." Because the other spies chose to put their faith in the circumstances that seemed contrary to God's promise, their report was, "We can't."

> But the men who had gone up with him said, "We are not able to go up against the people, for they are stronger than we." And they gave the children of Israel a bad report of the land which they had spied out, saying, "The land through which we have gone as spies is a land that devours its inhabitants, and all the people whom we saw in it are men of great stature. There we saw the giants (the descendants of Anak came from the giants); and we were like grasshoppers in our own sight, and so we were in their sight." (Numbers 13:31-33)

There's a lot that could be said here about the "psychology" of unbelief. Moments before, they were boasting about the fruitfulness of the land, but when confronted with a challenge to their faith, they quailed. Instead of seeing themselves in the light of

God's Word, as Caleb did, they hung onto their old image as slaves and conquered people.

They even projected this image onto the giants whom they had seen, "…and we were like grasshoppers…in their sight." How did they know that? Where did that conviction come from? I doubt they went down and polled the inhabitants of the land to see how they viewed the children of Israel. "Excuse me, Mr. Giant, but could you answer a few questions for us? How do you see us: a) conquering invaders, b) little people with a big God, or c) little grasshoppers?" No, this was their fears speaking to them!

This is why some people reject the Gospel today. They can't see themselves living in the grace and forgiveness God offers through Christ. They hang on to the image their past has created for them and reject the new life that God offers. God wanted His promise to give them a new identity of who they could be in Him, just as we who believe the Gospel are to no longer identify with the person we *were*, but with our new identity in Christ.

Therefore, from now on, we regard no one according to the flesh (the old man or woman they were before Christ)… Therefore, if anyone is in Christ, he is a *new creation*; old things have passed away; behold, *all things have become new*. (2 Corinthians 5:16-17)

Later, when Joshua sent his two men into the land to spy out Jericho, we find just how wrong the children of Israel were in their estimation of how the inhabitants of the land saw them. Rahab, the harlot, hid the spies on the roof of her house, and confided in them that the people of Jericho greatly feared the children of Israel.

Now before they lay down, she came up to them on the roof, and said to the men: "I know that the Lord has given you the land, that the terror of you has fallen on us, and that all the inhabitants of the land are fainthearted because of you. For we have heard how the Lord dried up the water of the Red Sea for you when you came out of Egypt, and what you did to the two kings of the Amorites who were on the other side of the Jordan, Sihon and Og, whom you utterly destroyed." (Joshua 2:8-10)

God had already been at work, preparing the way for the children of Israel, striking fear into the hearts of their adversaries, but instead of boldly going forth in faith to take what God had given them, their unbelief caused them to shrink back and forfeit their inheritance.

Interestingly, both Caleb and the other spies got what they believed. Forty years later, when this unbelieving generation was dead and buried, a new generation under Joshua's leadership, was ready to step up to the plate and act on the promise of God. The spies who had said that they could not go up and possess the Promised Land were all buried in the wilderness, their graves a vivid testimony to their refusal to believe and obey God. Caleb, on the other hand, was still there and ready to take his portion of the promise.

Then the children of Judah came to Joshua in Gilgal. And Caleb the son of Jephunneh the Kenizzite said to him: "You know the word which the Lord said to Moses the man of God concerning you and me in Kadesh Barnea. I was forty years old when Moses the servant of the Lord sent me from

Kadesh Barnea to spy out the land, and I brought back word to him as it was in my heart. Nevertheless my brethren who went up with me made the heart of the people melt, but I wholly followed the Lord my God. (Joshua 14:6-8)

Caleb had believed the promise of God, and that promise did not let him down. The power in the promise not only provided Caleb with an inheritance, but kept him strong until the time he could take possession.

And now, behold, the Lord has kept me alive, as He said, these forty-five years, ever since the Lord spoke this word to Moses while Israel wandered in the wilderness; and now, here I am this day, eighty-five years old. As yet I am as strong this day as on the day that Moses sent me; just as my strength was then, so now is my strength for war, both for going out and for coming in. Now therefore, give me this mountain of which the Lord spoke in that day; for you heard in that day how the Anakim were there, and that the cities were great and fortified. It may be that the Lord will be with me, and I shall be able to drive them out as the Lord said. (Joshua 14:10-12)

This is *faith talk!* This is what it sounds like when someone chooses to believe God's Word over any and all contradictory circumstances. Caleb meditated and incubated that promise in his heart all those years while he had to wander the wilderness with those who chose to forfeit their blessing through unbelief.

The important thing to notice is that the difference between those who failed to possess what God promised and Caleb had nothing to do with the promise of God, but had *everything* to do with their *response* to His promise. God's Word works, and the Gospel's saving power is available to anyone who will *mix faith* with it!

So, bringing it back to where we live, what does it really mean to *believe*? Most people in America today will say they believe in God. Many will even say they believe in Jesus, but don't go any further than acknowledging Him as a real historical person who did good works. So what does the Bible mean when it says we must *believe?*

There is much confusion in the world about what it really means to be a *believer*, or to be a Christian. Most know that Christians believe the Bible, but are a little vague on how that faith really affects their lives. Many believe being a Christian is about going to church and trying to live a good, moral life, while treating others in the same manner they would want to be treated. All good things, to be sure, but being a Christian and truly believing the Gospel does not begin with our attempts to *do* anything, but rather in our *believing* in what Christ did for us.

Again, it seems like everyone believes in God. Polls routinely show a high percentage of Americans who *believe* in God. Notice what this scripture says to the one who professes this kind of belief in God:

> You believe that there is one God. You do well. Even the demons believe—and tremble! (James 2:19)

James is saying that a mere intellectual acknowledgment of God might be a good place to start, but it's not the kind of believing that changes or transforms a life. Even the demons have that part down! Notice what he goes on to say.

> But do you want to know, O foolish man, that faith without works is dead? (James 2:20)

James is not saying that we have to supplement faith with good deeds to earn our salvation. The scriptures are clear that salvation, in any form, is a gift of the grace of God and not one we can earn by any effort or good works (see Ephesians 2:8, 9). Rather, what James is saying is that real believing puts feet to its faith! A faith that refuses to act on what it believes is not real Bible faith at all.

> What does it profit, my brethren, if someone says he has faith but does not have works? Can faith save him? (James 2:14)

Look at this in the *New Living Translation.*

> What good is it, dear brothers and sisters, if you say you have faith but don't show it by your *actions*? Can that kind of faith save anyone? (James 2:14, NLT)

James here is contrasting mere intellectual assent, which many call faith, with *real* Bible faith, which always follows what it believes with corresponding actions. It's the latter kind of faith rather than the former that *saves.* One who truly believes the Gospel doesn't just say, "Oh yes, I believe in Jesus," but he *acts* on what he hears, personally appropriating the grace of forgiveness and promise of eternal life for himself.

For God so loved the world that He gave His only begotten Son, *that whoever believes in Him should not perish but have everlasting life.* (John 3:16)

When we hear the Gospel, it produces faith in our hearts. As Paul says, "So then faith comes by hearing, and hearing by the word of God," (Romans 10:17). At that point, it's our choice whether we accept or reject the grace of God extended to us through Jesus Christ. It's a "whosoever will" proposition.

I have heard many stories of people who heard the Gospel of salvation and believed that what they heard was true, but refused to surrender to Christ because of either peer pressure or a reluctance to repent and abandon their sinful ways. Some have literally held on to the pew in front of them with a white-knuckled grip during an invitation to accept Christ, for fear their convicted heart would drag them down front to the altar to make Jesus Lord.

Did they believe? Yes, in one sense. But *that* kind of faith, that refuses to follow up with corresponding action, is not *saving* faith.

That if you confess with your mouth the Lord Jesus and believe in your heart that God has raised Him from the dead, you will be saved. For with the heart one believes unto righteousness, and with the mouth confession is made unto salvation. (Romans 10:9-10)

This passage from Romans is where we get the basis for what we often call the "sinner's prayer." When someone believes the Gospel, their faith demands that they *act* on what they hear and personally appropriate its promise for themselves. Often, we will help candidates who have heard and believed the Gospel to act on their faith by leading them in a prayer to accept Jesus as Lord. It's not a formula or magical set of phrases that saves them. In fact, the exact words are not really the issue. It is the communication of their heart's faith toward God and their *response* to the Gospel.

Years ago, in Bible school, I heard an excellent story that illustrates this point. A Pentecostal missionary on a Native American reservation, a woman, was preaching in the mission one night when a large, notoriously dangerous local Indian came into the building in the middle of her message. He was well-known for getting drunk and getting into fights, often taking on several policemen at a time. Everyone on the reservation feared him. The missionary herself feared he had come to the mission that night to disturb the meeting, but the large man merely sat in the service listening to the message.

As the service wound down to a close, the Pentecostal missionary gave an "altar call" for those who wished to accept Jesus into their lives and be saved. To her amazement, the large Indian started toward the front. At first, the woman missionary thought her worst fears were about to be realized, and that the giant Indian was going to start trouble. Instead of causing a disturbance, however, he got on his knees at the altar and began to cry out, "JESUS! JESUS! JESUS! JESUS!"

Finally, after the initial shock wore off, the missionary realized that this notoriously dangerous sinner was calling out to God for salvation. She quickly knelt down at the altar to help him "find his way to God." However, about the time she knelt beside him, he stood up to his full height, towering over the small Pentecostal woman. Her fears returned as she thought he might have changed his mind and decided instead to cause a scene.

She urged him to get down in the altar so that his sins could be washed away. "No need," he replied, "I'm saved." She protested, knowing what a sinful life this man had lived, thinking that surely someone who had been as wicked as he would need more time to get his heart right with God.

Frustrated with her attempts to get him back to the altar, he finally told her, "You have been preaching that 'whoever calls on the name of the Lord shall be saved,'" he said, referencing her text from Romans 10:13, "and I have called on Him four times!"

Surprised, this woman missionary realized that this ignorant, formerly violent sinner, had believed her message more than she had. While she had been trying to get him to "pray his way through to God," he had gotten through in a moment by simply acting on the childlike faith in his heart. The change in his life was immediately evident to all, and he went on to be an assistant to her in the work of the mission.

As we will see in later chapters, this same process of hearing, believing, and acting on the Word of God is the same one that secures salvation in every area of life. Our faith is *crucial* to releasing the Gospel's saving power.

Chapter 6

FROM DEATH
UNTO LIFE

We have seen that the Gospel is inherently powerful to save when one believes, acting on what they hear by faith. It is not enough to intellectually acknowledge that Jesus died for our sins, one must *respond* to the message and personally appropriate the promise in order for the saving power of the Gospel to be released. This is true, not only in the context of *spiritual* salvation, where the sinner must confess the lordship of Jesus, repent of his sins, and turn wholeheartedly toward God (see Romans 10:9, 10; Acts 2:38, 39), but in every other dimension of salvation as well.

Remember that C.I. Scofield, in his famous definition of the word, *salvation,* said, "The Hebrew and Greek words for 'salvation' imply the ideas of deliverance, safety, preservation, healing and soundness..."[2] The same Gospel that has power to save us inwardly or *spiritually* in the new birth has the power to heal us outwardly or *physically* as well. Again, the salvation God has provided for us is comprehensive, addressing every need we have now or could ever have.

However, before we move on, I believe it's important to understand the dynamics at work in the new birth and to see how God works in the hearts of individuals to literally change their natures when they surrender their hearts to Christ. Too often, the new birth is mistaken for "making a decision to be a better person" or "turning over a new leaf," as though the change was the result of making a New Year's resolution or some other commitment to improve oneself. Often, church attendance is perceived as merely a support system to help the newly committed hold fast to their resolution, in the same way members of Alcoholics Anonymous attend meetings to keep fresh their determination not to drink.

These views may be understandable from an outsider's perspective, especially if they have seen an individual make more than one attempt to change the course of his or her life through such natural means. They may see their friend or family member's newfound faith as the latest in a series of efforts to transform himself or herself. However, such views of the new birth fall far short of the truth and reduce a supernatural work of God to something accomplished through mere human effort or willpower. The new birth is affected by neither, nor does it produce a "better man," but rather a *brand new* person!

> Therefore, if anyone is in Christ, he is a new creation; old things have passed away; behold, all things have become new. (2 Corinthians 5:17)

The new birth is not a change of mind or a resolution reinforced by willpower. The new birth is just that, a *spiritual rebirth* or *re-creation* that produces a brand new man, not outwardly or physically, but inwardly or spiritually. Notice the same verse cited above, in *The Living Bible*:

> When someone becomes a Christian, he becomes a brand new person **inside**. He is not the same anymore. A new life has begun! (2 Corinthians 5:17, *The Living Bible*)

It was Jesus Himself who introduced this term, "born again," to describe this inward, spiritual change. The idea of a birth, or *rebirth*, was not merely used as a metaphor to illustrate a point, but as a very literal term to describe the inward, spiritual transformation that occurs within the *spirit* of the believer. We will see terminology used throughout the New Testament that reinforces this idea of a spiritual birth.

> There was a man of the Pharisees named Nicodemus, a ruler of the Jews. This man came to Jesus by night and said to Him, "Rabbi, we know that You are a teacher come from God; for no one can do these signs that You do unless God is with him."
>
> Jesus answered and said to him, "Most assuredly, I say to you, unless one is born again, he cannot see the kingdom of God."
>
> Nicodemus said to Him, "How can a man be born when he is old? Can he enter a second time into his mother's womb and be born?"
>
> Jesus answered, "Most assuredly, I say to you, unless one is born of water and the Spirit, he cannot enter the kingdom of God. That which is born of the flesh is flesh, and that which is born of the Spirit is spirit." (John 3:1-6)

Even to the casual reader, it should be obvious that Jesus is contrasting two different kinds of birth; one physical, the other spiritual. Just as we are born into this *natural* life, we have to be born again or born of God to have *spiritual* life and entrance into the Kingdom of God.

Until one is born into this natural, physical world, he can't see or perceive the things of this world. They're not accessible to him, thus he is unable to grasp or comprehend them. Likewise, until one is born again, he is an alien to the Kingdom of God. He cannot perceive spiritual things because he is not alive to spiritual reality. Spiritual things are an enigma to the natural man.

But the natural man does not receive the things of the Spirit of God, for they are foolishness to him; nor can he know them, because they are spiritually discerned. But he who is spiritual judges all things, yet he himself is rightly judged by no one. (1 Corinthians 2:14-15)

It is very trendy today to say, "I am spiritual, but not religious," usually meaning they are open to spiritual things but not into organized religion. But the truth is, until a person is born again, all he or she *can* be is religious. After all, there are many religions or systems of belief in the world which have nothing to do with the Bible. However, according to God's Word, one cannot be truly *spiritual* until he or she is born again.

The *natural* man, as he is referred to here, is one who has been born naturally, or born into this physical world, but not yet born again or born of God. The *spiritual* man is the one who has been born again by the Spirit of God. As we have seen already, that rebirth was a *spiritual* birth by which one is brought into the

Kingdom of God. That realm of spiritual reality is now opened to him and he can perceive and understand spiritual things.

> But people who aren't spiritual *(who don't have the Spirit; or who have only physical life)* can't receive these truths from God's Spirit. It all sounds foolish to them and they can't understand it, for only those who are spiritual can understand what the Spirit means. Those who are spiritual can evaluate all things, but they themselves cannot be evaluated by others. (1 Corinthians 2:14-15, NLT)

To fully understand these truths, we must understand that God made man a triune being; spirit, soul, and body (see 1 Thessalonians 5:23, 24). Actually, man is a spirit being who possesses a soul (mind, will and emotions) and lives in a physical "house" called a body. Too often, we have focused on only the physical, intellectual, or emotional aspects of man and skipped over the spiritual component of our being all together. Today, there are thousands of self-help books for maintaining one's mental health, managing one's emotions, or getting physically fit, but the world still knows little to nothing of how to fix man's spiritual problem. The reason for this is that the answer can only be found in the Word of God. Jesus gave the solution in five words: "You must be born again" (John 3:7).

As we've already seen, we've all been born into Adam, and thus, into sin. When Adam rebelled against God's authority in the Garden of Eden, eating the forbidden fruit of the tree of the knowledge of good and evil, he died spiritually.

> And the Lord God commanded the man, saying, "Of every tree of the garden you may freely eat; but of the tree of the

knowledge of good and evil you shall not eat, for in the day
that you eat of it you shall surely die." (Genesis 2:16-17)

God warned Adam that in the very day he ate of the fruit he
would die, and yet we know that Adam went on to live for nine
hundred and thirty years! How do we reconcile this?

The answer is in understanding that the Bible speaks of three
kinds of death: physical death, spiritual death, and the second
death. To most of us, death means "the cessation of life," but in the
Bible, death never means that. Rather, death means *separation.*

In physical death, the spirit is separated from the body, which
is laid to rest in the ground. The spirit, however, immediately goes
to one of two destinations; Heaven or Hades, the place of departed
spirits. There is no such thing as "soul sleep," as some religions
teach. Instead, the Bible teaches clearly that when we die physically,
our eternal spirit arrives immediately in the place we chose by
virtue of our acceptance or rejection of the grace of God in Christ
(fully aware and fully conscious of our surroundings).

Jesus said to the thief on the cross, who in his dying moments
recognized and confessed the lordship of Jesus, "Assuredly, I say to
you, *today* you will be with Me in Paradise" (Luke 23:43). Likewise,
in the story of the rich man and Lazarus, both were wide awake and
fully conscious in their respective places; Lazarus in Abraham's
bosom (Paradise), and the rich man in torment in Hades. Their
memories of their earthly lives were intact as was their awareness of
those still living (see Luke 16:19-31).

Now, on this side of the cross, in the New Covenant, those
who depart this natural life in Christ go to be with the Lord (see
2 Corinthians 5:8; Philippians 1:23). Paradise is no longer in the

heart of the earth, separated from Hades by a gulf, as in the story of the rich man and Lazarus. When Christ was raised from the dead, He led to heaven those spirits who were in that place of comfort in Abraham's bosom (see Ephesians 4:6). It is those saints – along with all who will depart to be with the Lord up until His return – who will come back with Him when the Church is caught up to meet the Lord in the air; an experience commonly known as the Rapture of the Church.

> For this we say to you by the word of the Lord, that we who are alive and remain until the coming of the Lord will by no means precede those who are asleep. For the Lord Himself will descend from heaven with a shout, with the voice of an archangel, and with the trumpet of God. And the dead in Christ will rise first. Then we who are alive and remain shall be caught up together with them in the clouds to meet the Lord in the air. And thus we shall always be with the Lord. Therefore comfort one another with these words.
> (1 Thessalonians 4:15-18)

For the one who dies in Christ, death holds no fear, as Paul tells us himself.

> So when this corruptible *(body)* has put on incorruption, and this mortal *(body)* has put on immortality, then shall be brought to pass the saying that is written: "Death is swallowed up in victory."
> "O Death, where is your sting? O Hades, where is your victory?" (1 Corinthians 15:54-55)

Death has no victory over the believer. It is the last enemy to be put underfoot (see 1 Corinthians 15:26), but to those of us who are in Christ, it is only a transition from this life to the next, which, as Paul says, is "far better" (Philippians 1:23). So grieve not overly much for those loved ones who have passed on in Christ. You will see them again if you are also in Christ, and the rejoicing from that reunion will never end.

Spiritual death occurs when one experiences separation from God through sin. This is the death Adam experienced when he sinned in the Garden of Eden, and *that* death – that spiritual separation from God – was passed on to all of us (see Romans 5:12). While Adam still lived physically for many years, he was immediately conscious of a separation from God, *spiritually*. In fact, both he and Eve tried to hide their sinful condition and shame by sewing fig leaves together. Their innocence had been lost forever and a consciousness of their sin and separation from God became dominant.

> Then the eyes of both of them were opened, and they knew that they were naked; and they sewed fig leaves together and made themselves coverings. And they heard the sound of the Lord God walking in the garden in the cool of the day, and Adam and his wife hid themselves from the presence of the Lord God among the trees of the garden. (Genesis 3:7-8)

Man's sin could not be covered by man's device. God clothed both Adam and Eve with the skin of an animal, an early prophetic picture that blood must be shed to cover man's fallen and sinful condition before God. It is, in fact, in this very chapter of Genesis that the first prophecy of Jesus coming as our Redeemer is found in Scripture. In the pronouncement of His curse over the serpent, God spoke the following judgment on Satan who had used the serpent's form.

> And I will put enmity
> Between you and the woman,
> And between your seed and her Seed;
> He shall bruise your head,
> And you shall bruise His heel. (Genesis 3:15)

Thousands of years later, on an old rugged cross on Golgotha's hill, Satan would bruise the heel of Christ, the seed of the woman, but ultimately it was Satan's head – his dominion and authority – that would be crushed by Christ's atoning sacrifice.

At that moment in the Garden of Eden, man stood naked, stripped of his innocence and separated from God by sin and spiritual death. It was there in the Garden that man lost the ability to stand blameless and without shame in the presence of a righteous God. That same sin consciousness that caused Adam to shrink away and hide from the presence of God has been passed down to all of his children.

> Therefore, just as through one man sin entered the world,
> and death through sin, and thus death spread to all men,
> because all sinned... (Romans 5:12)

Adam was our representative in the Garden. We were all "in him," so to speak. Thus, spiritual death and the resulting sin nature were passed on to us through Adam's fall. All this talk of man being inherently good is unbiblical. Man is a fallen creature with a fallen nature. Notice how Jesus addressed the crowds in His day that tried to lay their claim to righteousness on the basis of their religious heritage, claiming Abraham as their father.

> You are of your father the devil, and the desires of your father you want to do. He was a murderer from the beginning, and does not stand in the truth, because there is no truth in him. When he speaks a lie, he speaks from his own resources, for he is a liar and the father of it. (John 8:44)

I like the *New International Version* of this verse which says, "When he lies, he speaks his *native language*, for he is a liar and the father of lies." The devil lies because it is his nature to do so, hence, it is his *native* language. Likewise, the devil's children, those who have his fallen nature, do deeds consistent with that nature.

We cannot expect sinners to live and act righteously any more than we can expect a cat to bark or a dog to climb trees. It's simply not in their nature. For a sinner to begin to act like a saint, he needs a new nature!

When we think of the devil's nature, we might think of heinous crimes against humanity or overt cruelty. Those are certainly the works of the devil, but the best word to sum up the fallen sin nature of the devil is *"self."* The sin nature, which all humanity shares through Adam's fall, is egocentric and seeks to gratify self and selfish desire. This nature is epitomized in the devil's rebellion against God and subsequent fall, described by the prophet Isaiah.

> How you are fallen from heaven,
> O Lucifer, son of the morning!
> How you are cut down to the ground,
> You who weakened the nations!

For you have said in your heart:
"I will ascend into heaven,
I will exalt my throne above the stars of God;
I will also sit on the mount of the congregation
On the farthest sides of the north;
I will ascend above the heights of the clouds,
I will be like the Most High."
Yet you shall be brought down to Sheol,
To the lowest depths of the Pit. (Isaiah 14:12-15)

If you followed them, there were five *I's* in those verses. Five times, Lucifer, the archangel who fell and became the devil, declared that he would exalt his ambitions against the will of God. Lucifer clearly had "I" trouble, and it cost him everything. Unfortunately, through man's fall, that same nature passed to Adam and consequently, to us.

All we like sheep have gone astray;
We have turned, every one, to *his own way*;
And the Lord has laid on Him the iniquity of us all.
(Isaiah 53:6)

All sin is selfish. No one sins and thinks that by so doing they are helping others. And sin always costs. In fact, "the wages of sin is death" (Romans 6:23). Not only does it cost the sinner, but those whom the selfish acts of the sinner affect. God hates sin but loves the sinner. He doesn't hate sin because He's a "killjoy" but because *sin kills* (see also Galatians 6:7-8).

Recall what Jesus said in the verse cited earlier, describing the devil's fallen nature.

You are of your father the devil, and the desires of your father you want to do. *He was a murderer from the beginning...* (John 8:44)

This verse used to bother me because I couldn't figure out what *beginning* Jesus was referring to when he said the devil "was a murderer from the beginning." Another passage of scripture sheds light on Jesus' meaning; a passage of scripture also penned by John in the first epistle that bears his name.

For this is the message that you heard from the beginning, that we should love one another, not as Cain *who was of the wicked one and murdered his brother.* And why did he murder him? Because his works were evil and his brother's righteous. (1 John 3:11-12)

This is just one generation after the fall of man and already we can see the sin nature fully matured and at work in Cain as he seeks to advance himself at his brother's expense. As we said, sin is selfish and always seeks to promote its own interests at the expense of others. The ultimate expression of this is murder. Today, our headlines are filled with unthinkable stories of murders committed against family members, even mothers killing their own children, to advance the murderers own selfish interests. As unbelievable as these stories are, they are consistent with the fallen nature we inherited from our father, Adam.

By contrast, the nature of God is love. The Bible says God *is* love (see 1 John 4:8, 16). Love always seeks to promote the interests of others, even at its own expense; the polar opposite of the selfish, sin nature. The ultimate expression of this love nature is to lay one's life down for another.

> Greater love has no one than this, than to lay down one's life for his friends. (John 15:13)

This nature was demonstrated in Christ's sacrifice for us, the greatest expression of this love the universe has ever witnessed.

> Therefore be imitators of God as dear children. And walk in love, *as Christ also has loved us and given Himself* for us, an offering and a sacrifice to God for a sweet-smelling aroma. (Ephesians 5:1-2)

Paul tells the Ephesian believers to imitate God and walk in this same love that Christ demonstrated in His sacrificial death. How could fallen beings ever hope to demonstrate the love of God as Jesus did? There's only one way, by being born again and receiving the life of God. Again, the power of God to accomplish this is in the Gospel.

> Having been born again, not of corruptible seed but incorruptible, through the word of God which lives and abides forever... (1 Peter 1:23)

We are born again through believing the Gospel, as we have explained before. But it is this word, "seed," in the above verse that is significant in the matter of a changed nature. It is the Greek word, *sperma*. This is *spiritual biology* at work, if you will.

When you were born, naturally speaking, it was the *seed* of your natural father that carried the genetic material that helped to make you the person you are today – *naturally* speaking. You are who you are and act like you do to a great degree because of the genes you received from your natural parents when you were formed in your mother's womb.

Some years ago, when I went back to Mississippi, some of my relatives on my dad's side of the family who hadn't seen me for many years commented on how much they could see my mother in me. (I often joke and say that it was the beard!)

Why did they say that? What was it they saw? I wasn't trying to act like my mother, and I certainly wasn't wearing her clothes! It wasn't anything conscious on my part at all. Since then, I have had others who knew my dad say that I remind them of him! Certain looks and mannerisms that they possessed just naturally found their expression in me. I simply have certain genetic predispositions because of who my parents are; because of the family I was born into.

Spiritually speaking, there are only two families in the earth today – the family of God and the family of the devil. Before we are born again, we follow the nature that our spiritual father, Adam, passed on to us – the nature of the devil. However, when you are born *again* you are literally "re-*gene*-erated." God changes your spiritual DNA! His incorruptible seed produces a new creation – a child of God!

> Not by works of righteousness which we have done, but according to His mercy He saved us, through the washing of *regeneration* and renewing of the Holy Spirit... (Titus 3:5)

That word "regeneration" is the Greek word *palingenesías* from the words *palin* (again) and *genesis,* (birth). It literally means *born again.* You can forget the former nature passed on to you from your father, Adam. Now you have a *new* Father who has given you a *new* nature. In fact, as we have already seen in verses we have looked at, we are "partakers of the *divine* nature" (2 Peter 2:4).

For too long, people in the world have justified certain lifestyles and sinful behavior by saying, "Well, I was born this way," thinking they were saying, "God made me this way." Absolutely not! God did not create man a fallen being. Man sinned and died spiritually, becoming alienated from the life and nature of God. Thus, the whole course of this world is governed by the devil, who controls men through their selfish passions and desires.

And you He made alive, who were dead in trespasses and sins, in which you once walked *according to the course of this world*, according to the *prince of the power of the air*, the spirit who now works in the sons of disobedience, among whom also we all once conducted ourselves in the lusts of our flesh, *fulfilling the desires of the flesh and of the mind*, and were by nature children of wrath, just as the others. (Ephesians 2:1-3)

The sin nature expresses itself in every natural man, though it may be expressed differently in each person, depending on influence and environment. However, regardless of one's particular proclivity to sin, we cannot justify those behaviors by saying, "I was born this way." Society cannot sanitize what the Bible calls sin by giving it "societal sanction." Rather, those sinful behaviors we are bound to because of our fallen nature ought to underscore our need for the Savior.

Again, we're not just dealing with a "sin" problem, but rather a "sinner" problem! Sinful *actions* proceed forth from a sin *nature*, but God will give you a *new* nature through Jesus Christ, and set you free from the power of sin in all its expressions!

> For the law of the Spirit of life in Christ Jesus has made me free from the law of sin and death. (Romans 8:2)

When one is born again and receives the nature of God, he is empowered by God to live a life victorious over sin. The Holy Spirit comes to live within him, to strengthen and guide him in this new life. In fact, the Bible teaches that it is impossible for the born-again child of God to live a life of habitual sin.

> Those who have been born into God's family do not make a practice of sinning, because God's life is in them. So they can't keep on sinning, because they are children of God. (1 John 3:9, NLT)

We all know Christians can still sin. That is no revelation to any of us who have been saved more than a day! However, the man or woman who has been born of God cannot live a life *given over* to sin because such a lifestyle is at variance with their nature. Notice this verse in the *Amplified Bible*.

> No one born (begotten) of God [deliberately, knowingly, and habitually] practices sin, for God's nature abides in him [His principle of life, the divine sperm, remains permanently within him]; and he cannot practice sinning because he is born (begotten) of God. (1 John 3:9, AMP)

As I've often said when referring to this verse: "A Christian can *deliberately* sin. A Christian can *knowingly* sin. But a true born-again child of God cannot deliberately, knowingly, *habitually practice* sin!" It is an unfortunate reality that any of us can postpone our growth and development in the Lord and fall back into routines of the flesh – even sins – that grieve the Spirit of God within us. This is not to condemn those who have missed it as a child of God. We've all missed it! But through the new birth and the indwelling Holy Spirit, God has given us the ability to rise above sin and experience total victory in Him!

The true Christian who is born of God *wants* to live right. However, the new birth is not the end of the story. It is, in fact, just the beginning, as is any birth. The believer must continue to grow and mature in the new life, through feeding on the Word of God and learning to control the desires of the flesh that are at work in the mortal body. The real outworking of our salvation and the visible transformation of our lives come as we renew our minds with the Word of God and present our bodies to God for His exclusive use (see Romans 12:1, 2). God has done the heavy lifting for us in changing our nature through the power of the Gospel and the work of the Holy Spirit. But it is our responsibility to change the way we think and exercise control over our flesh.

Remember, we are not in this alone! Not only will the Lord help us personally, through our own devotional life, but also as we participate in a growing, thriving, local church family. This is all part of God's recipe to help us build strong spiritual lives. The Word is clear that we need each other to grow into the people God has called us to be (see Hebrews 10:24, 25; Ephesians 4:11-16). It is in the local church that we find opportunities to grow through our connections with others, as well as opportunities to serve, using the spiritual gifts He has given to each one of us (see Romans 12:3-6; Ephesians 4:7; 1 Peter 4:10, 11).

There are two more things that we should point out before closing this chapter. First, when talking about spiritual death and our being born into sin through our natural father, Adam, we do not want to cause alarm in the hearts of those who have tragically lost infants or young children before they accepted Jesus as Savior. The Bible is very clear that, "where there is no law there is no transgression" (Romans 4:15), and a baby or young child who doesn't know the difference between right and wrong (as represented by the law) cannot transgress. Paul discusses this issue in his epistle to the Romans.

I was alive once without the law, but when the commandment came, sin revived and I died. (Romans 7:9)

Paul is saying that before the knowledge of the law (the knowledge of right and wrong) came to him, he was alive to God. However, when the time came that he knew to do right and failed to do it, he transgressed the law of God and died spiritually.

That age at which we come to know the difference between right and wrong is often referred to as "the age of accountability," and it differs from person to person, depending on things like one's spiritual influences and environment. For example, someone who grew up in a Christian home, exposed to the Word of God, might come to that age of accountability much more quickly than someone who grew up ignorant of spiritual things. The important thing to understand is that no child, innocent of the knowledge of right from wrong, is lost. If such a child dies, his or her spirit would immediately go to be with the Lord.

The second thing we should mention is what the Bible teaches concerning the third kind of death. It is called the second death and refers to the eternal separation from God that those who reject the grace of God will suffer as they are cast into the Lake of Fire, forever lost.

> Then I saw a great white throne and Him who sat on it, from whose face the earth and the heaven fled away. And there was found no place for them. And I saw the dead, small and great, standing before God, and books were opened. And another book was opened, which is the Book of Life. And the dead were judged according to their works, by the things which were written in the books. The sea gave up the dead who were in it, and Death and Hades delivered up the dead who were in them. And they were judged, each one according to his works. Then Death and Hades were cast into the lake of fire. This is the second death. And anyone not found written in the Book of Life was cast into the lake of fire. (Revelation 20:11-15)

This judgment is commonly known as the Great White Throne Judgment. It is the final judgment of those who rejected the Gospel and refused the grace of God in Christ. This is not the Judgment Seat of Christ, which is the judgment of the believer. Paul refers to this in the epistles (1 Corinthians 3:12-15; 2 Corinthians 5:10, 11). To put it succinctly, no one who appears at the Great White Throne of Judgment will go to Heaven, and no one who appears at the Judgment Seat of Christ will go to Hell.

The Judgment Seat of Christ is where rewards are determined for believers according to their faithfulness to God's will for their lives here on earth. The Great White Throne of Judgment is where those who rejected Christ will hear their final doom and experience eternal separation from the presence of God in a place intended, not for man, but for the devil and his angels (see Matthew 25:41). Not only is our nature determined by the family we're in, but ultimately our judgment also. Those who are members of God's family will experience life in His presence where there is fullness of joy (Psalm 16:11), while those who die members of the devil's family will share in the everlasting torment God has prepared for him.

While these are truly sobering realities, they should underscore the seriousness of every man's response to the Gospel. Further, they should underscore the seriousness of our responsibility as believers to make the most of every opportunity to share our faith, both in what we say and how we demonstrate the power of the Gospel in our lives. Seeing the horrible judgment that awaits those who die in their sin, we can understand why God would be willing to go to the ultimate lengths to save us, not when we were at our best, but when we were at our worst.

> But God demonstrates His own love toward us, in that while we were still sinners, Christ died for us. (Romans 5:8)

Jesus hung on Calvary's cruel cross, innocent in Himself, yet bearing all our guilt and shame so that the scales of divine justice would be balanced, erasing our debt before the throne of God. God's wrath was poured out completely, once for all time, on His Son who became our substitute and bore our judgment (see Isaiah 53). Now, through His sacrifice, life is available where death once reigned, and the throne of judgment has become a throne of grace for all who will believe.

Chapter 7

THE GOSPEL'S HEALING POWER

> How God anointed Jesus of Nazareth with the Holy Spirit
> and with power, who went about doing good and healing
> all who were oppressed by the devil, for God was with Him.
> (Acts 10:38)

We've seen again and again that the Gospel is the "power of
God unto *salvation*" (Romans 1:16), which includes deliverance,
safety, preservation, *healing* and soundness. In fact, the salvation
God provided us through the finished work of Christ is a *complete*
salvation that covers every need in life, and prepares us for the life
to come.

While we in the Church have tended to understand the words
"salvation" and "saved" to refer primarily to spiritual salvation, the
Greek words (soteria and sozo, respectively), have a broader
meaning which includes the full range of God's deliverance from
sin. In fact, as we turn our attention to the Gospel's power to heal,

we'll see in particular that this word, *sozo*, translated "save" or "saved," is often used to refer to physical deliverance or healing.

In fact, the Greek word translated "power" here in Romans 1:16, *dunamis*, is the same Greek word translated "power" in Acts 10:38, mentioned above. In other words, just as Jesus, the *Living* Word, was anointed to heal, so too is the *inspired* Word of the Gospel. The Gospel is anointed to heal because the Gospel includes healing. This will be made irrefutably clear as we proceed.

First, however, we will take a look at some of the passages where the Greek word *sozo* or "saved" was used in connection with healing. To begin, we'll take a look at two stories from the life of Jesus as recorded in Mark's Gospel.

Now a certain woman had a flow of blood for twelve years, and had suffered many things from many physicians. She had spent all that she had and was no better, but rather grew worse. When she heard about Jesus, she came behind Him in the crowd and touched His garment. For she said, "If only I may touch His clothes, I shall be made well."

Immediately the fountain of her blood was dried up, and she felt in her body that she was healed of the affliction. And Jesus, immediately knowing in Himself that power had gone out of Him, turned around in the crowd and said, "Who touched My clothes?"

But His disciples said to Him, "You see the multitude thronging You, and You say, 'Who touched Me?'"

And He looked around to see her who had done this thing. But the woman, fearing and trembling, knowing what had happened to her, came and fell down before Him and told

Him the whole truth. And He said to her, "Daughter, your faith has made you well. Go in peace, and be healed of your affliction." (Mark 5:25-34)

It is important to see in this account that just as faith in the Gospel releases God's saving power in the context of the new birth, the same is true when it comes to the Gospel's *healing* power. First of all, notice how this story begins.

When she heard about Jesus, she came behind Him in the crowd and touched His garment. (Mark 5:27)

After understanding the back story of this woman's seemingly incurable condition, we see that the real catalyst of her determination to be healed was *hearing* the "good news" of what Jesus was doing. We saw that the good news of the Promised Land constituted a "Gospel" for the children of Israel that would have produced great blessing, had they believed it. Here too we will see the power of God being released as this woman believes and acts on the good news she heard.

This woman's faith was expressed and revealed in two particular things she did. Verse 27 says, "...she came behind Him in the crowd and touched his garment...," but even this act of faith was preceded by something else.

When she heard about Jesus, she came behind Him in the crowd and touched His garment. *For she said*, "If only I may touch His clothes, I shall be made well." (Mark 5:27-28)

Her faith was demonstrated first in what she *said*, and then in what she *did*. To put it in terms we looked at in regard to spiritual salvation; she believed in her heart and confessed with her mouth (see Romans 10:9-10). In other words, this was not mere wishful thinking, it was faith in action. Her confession of faith was also followed by something even more daring.

As a Jewish woman in a Jewish culture, it was not lawful for her to be in public with an issue of blood. The book of Leviticus contains detailed instructions on the sequestering of such a person. However, hers was a faith that would not be denied. She cast all hesitation aside and made her way, inch by inch, through that crowd to touch the hem of Jesus' garment. Notice what Kenneth Wuest's excellent translation says about this crowd that was pressing about Jesus.

> And there kept on following with Him a large crowd, and they kept on pressing upon Him almost to the point of suffocation. (Mark 5:24, *The New Testament: An Expanded Translation*)

The point here is that her convictions ran so deep that she was willing to push through a very tightly pressed crowd to get her healing. I'm sure there were others in the vicinity who needed healing of similar or even worse conditions, but the Bible says nothing about anyone else in this crowd getting a thing. What was different about her? She *believed!*

Notice what happened when this woman decided to act on the good news she believed with all her heart.

> Immediately the fountain of her blood was dried up, and she felt in her body that she was healed of the affliction. And Jesus, immediately knowing in Himself that power

had gone out of Him, turned around in the crowd and said, "Who touched My clothes?" (Mark 5:29-30)

If you look closely, you'll see that the woman was conscious of her healing and Jesus was conscious of the anointing or power going out of Him. Her faith put a demand on the power! When teaching and preaching along these lines, we'll often say, "Faith gives action to the power." This is certainly true, as seen in this account.

Jesus stopped and turned to see who it was who made contact with the anointing. Faith gets God's attention. The famous English evangelist, Smith Wigglesworth, was famous for saying, "There's something about faith that will cause God to skip over a million people just to bless you." It's true. God is moved with compassion, but He's moved *by* faith! If God were merely moved by desperation, He would be moving in the lives of billions of people on the planet. But though God loves and cares for each and every human and wants to heal the hurts of the whole world, the Scripture is clear in showing us that God is moved, and His power released, when we believe.

While the disciples were trying to understand what Jesus was asking, He was looking for the person whose faith made a connection with the power of God. What is truly amazing in this story – and so contrary to most of our religious conditioning – is where Jesus laid the credit for her healing.

But the woman, fearing and trembling, knowing what had happened to her, came and fell down before Him and told Him the whole truth. And He said to her, "Daughter, *your faith* has made you well. Go in peace, and be healed of your affliction." (Mark 5:33-34)

We've all looked at stories like this one in the Gospels and said things like, "Isn't it wonderful how Jesus healed that woman? He can do that, you know. After all, He's the Son of God!" While Jesus *is* the divine Son of God, His ministry was *not* carried out *as* the Son of God. Jesus became a man to identify with us, and as such, He laid aside the inherent power He possessed as the second person of the Godhead and became a man like you and me.

> But (Jesus) stripped Himself [of all privileges and rightful dignity], so as to assume the guise of a servant (slave), in that He became like men and was born a human being. (Philippians 2:7, AMP)

> When the time came, he set aside the privileges of deity and took on the status of a slave, became human! Having become human, he stayed human. It was an incredibly humbling process. He didn't claim special privileges. (Philippians 2:7-8, MSG)

Remember the verse we saw at the very beginning of this chapter.

> How God anointed Jesus of Nazareth with the Holy Spirit and with power, who went about doing good and healing all who were oppressed by the devil, for God was with Him. (Acts 10:38)

If Jesus had been performing the miracles He did as God, then why would He need to be anointed by the Holy Spirit? The second person of the Godhead certainly has all the power of the third person, the Holy Spirit. And yet, Jesus was anointed by God with the Holy Spirit, and with power. Had He not been, and performed

His miracles as the divine Son of God, we could never reproduce them. Yet He clearly told His disciples that they (and we) would reproduce and even surpass the things He did!

> Most assuredly, I say to you, he who believes in Me, the works that I do he will do also; *and greater works than these* he will do, because I go to My Father. (John 14:12)

When Jesus ascended to be seated at the right hand of the Father, He gave the Church the same Spirit and power with which He was anointed, that we might continue His works.

> How God anointed Jesus of Nazareth with the *Holy Spirit and with power...* (Acts 10:38)

> But you shall receive *power* when the *Holy Spirit* has come upon you... (Acts 1:8)

That word *power* in Acts 1:8 is exactly the same word translated "power" in all the other verses we've looked at so far. In fact, it's the same word translated "power" in Mark 5:33, where Jesus felt "power" go out of Him into the woman with the issue of blood. In other words, just as Jesus was anointed to heal by the Spirit of God upon Him, so too we can do the same works through the power of the Holy Spirit upon us. Not only that, but we have the Gospel which is anointed with healing power!

> And these signs will follow those who believe: In My name they will....lay hands on the sick, and they will recover. (Mark 16:17-18)

This power with which Jesus was anointed, responded to the woman's faith when she believed what she heard. Jesus said, "Daughter, *your faith* has made you well." The anointing of the Holy Spirit was there for everyone in that crowd. God is no respecter of persons. But God's power responds to the one who believes.

Lastly, notice one particular part of this last verse:

And He said to her, "Daughter, your faith has *made you well.* Go in peace, and be healed of your affliction." (Mark 5:34)

Those words "made you well" are actually translated from the Greek word *sozo* or "saved." Jesus actually said to this woman, "Your faith has *saved* you." Again, God's power to save includes healing just as much as it does spiritual salvation! If this woman received healing through her faith when she believed what she heard, then we can certainly receive when we likewise believe!

Let's turn to a different account and see the same principle of faith in action, releasing God's healing power.

Now they came to Jericho. As He went out of Jericho with His disciples and a great multitude, blind Bartimaeus, the son of Timaeus, sat by the road begging. And when he heard that it was Jesus of Nazareth, he began to cry out and say, "Jesus, Son of David, have mercy on me!"

Then many warned him to be quiet; but he cried out all the more, "Son of David, have mercy on me!"

So Jesus stood still and commanded him to be called.

Then they called the blind man, saying to him, "Be of good cheer. Rise, He is calling you."

And throwing aside his garment, he rose and came to Jesus.

So Jesus answered and said to him, "What do you want Me to do for you?"

The blind man said to Him, "Rabboni, that I may receive my sight."

Then Jesus said to him, "Go your way; your faith has made you well." And immediately he received his sight and followed Jesus on the road. (Mark 10:46-52)

Both the woman healed of the issue of blood and Bartimaeus are excellent examples of tenacious faith; faith that so believes, it simply will not be denied. It seems obvious, judging from Bartimaeus' reaction to hearing that it was Jesus who was walking by, that he had heard of Him before. In fact, his reaction indicates that he had heard things similar to those that had inspired the faith of the woman healed in the last story we read.

Whatever he had heard about Jesus, there's no question about the fact that he immediately began to demonstrate a very determined faith.

And when he heard that it was Jesus of Nazareth, he began to cry out and say, "Jesus, Son of David, have mercy on me!"

Then many warned him to be quiet; but he cried out all the more, "Son of David, have mercy on me!" (Mark 10:47-48)

This man, being blind, couldn't make his way as directly to Jesus as could the woman suffering from the issue of blood. His best chance was to get Jesus' attention by causing a ruckus! Just as in most churches, his ruckus-causing faith was not appreciated by the crowd. But this man was willing to set etiquette and decorum on its head to get his healing! And again, faith made Heaven take notice.

So Jesus stood still and commanded him to be called. (Mark 10:49)

We need to realize that Jesus did not just act on His own initiative. He said again and again, in one way or another, "I have come down from heaven, not to do My own will, but the will of Him who sent Me" (John 6:38). Jesus was the will of God in motion, if you will (see John 1:18; Hebrews 1:3). He came to reveal the Father to us. If faith moved Jesus, and determined who received from Him, it should be a lesson to us on what moves God now. He never changes (see Hebrews 13:8).

It's interesting that once Jesus called for Bartimaeus, the entire crowd was behind him saying: "Be of good cheer. Rise. He is calling you." All of us want the testimony. Everybody rejoices at faith's great victories, but we have to realize that sometimes the very people who will praise God for our victories once they are won, are the very ones who will tell us to keep calm and not go over the deep end when we're in the middle of our faith fight. They don't want us to cause a ruckus! Sometimes to get the *testimony*, we have to endure in the *test*.

What follows in this story is a beautiful picture of faith in motion. Upon hearing that Jesus was calling for him, Bartimaeus cast aside his garment and shed his old life as a blind beggar to gain a new one as a man about to receive his sight.

And throwing aside his garment, he rose and came to Jesus.
(Mark 10:50)

It is said that the outer garment of the blind was used as
bedding at night as well as a collection receptacle for any alms
thrown their way as they sat begging beside the lanes of commerce.
When Bartimaeus cast his garment aside, it was to say, "Enough of
this beggar's life. I'm about to start climbing up in life!"

While Jesus' next question might seem obvious to some and
even insensitive to others, it is perfectly understandable when
one understands the discouraging affects of long-standing sickness or disability.

So Jesus answered and said to him, "What do you want Me
to do for you?" The blind man said to Him, "Rabboni, that
I may receive my sight." (Mark 10:51)

There are those who have so learned to accommodate sickness
and disease in their lives that any hope of a change has long left
them. Indeed, they may consider harboring a hope of change for
the better as a dangerous thing. They have learned to live with their
condition and accept it. They have made peace with it. However,
Jesus did not come to make peace with any of the devil's works.

For this purpose the Son of God was manifested, that He
might destroy the works of the devil. (1 John 3:8)

Sickness and disease are physical manifestations of the spiritual
death that came into the human experience through Adam's transgression. As the late John Alexander Dowie is quoted as saying,

"Sickness is the foul offspring of its father, Satan, and its mother, Sin." The ultimate remedy for all the works of sin and Satan was the cross where Christ forever released us from these cruel, twin taskmasters. The same verse we saw earlier that showed us that it was God who anointed Jesus to heal the sick, also shows us that Satan is the oppressor and author of sickness.

> How God anointed Jesus of Nazareth with the Holy Spirit and with power, who went about doing good and healing all *who were oppressed by the devil*, for God was with Him. (Acts 10:38)

Bartimaeus' expressed desire to have his sight shows that nothing had put his faith to rest. It was still alive, active, and full of hope for a better day. He had incessantly cried out for mercy. When confronted with the opportunity to receive mercy from the Master, it came in the form of healing for his blind eyes.

Jesus did not argue with his request for mercy to be expressed in the form of physical healing, but said instead, "Go your way; *your faith has made you whole.*" This is encouraging since we are told to "come boldly to the throne of grace, that we may obtain *mercy*…in time of need" (Hebrews 4:16). His healing mercies are still there for you and me because the blood of Jesus still testifies to the full salvation He provided when He obtained eternal redemption for us.

Again, the words, "made you well" in verse 54 are translated from the word *sozo* or "saved," proving once again that the power of God to save includes healing, and is obtained by faith in the same way we believe and are born again. God will save you *inside and out* when you believe His Word.

In the epistle of James to the dispersed Jewish believers, we read instructions for the sick one who wants to obtain God's saving power for the body.

> Is anyone among you sick? Let him call for the elders of the church, and let them pray over him, anointing him with oil in the name of the Lord. And the prayer of faith will save the sick, and the Lord will raise him up. And if he has committed sins, he will be forgiven. (James 5:14-15)

The word "save" in verse 15 is again the Greek word *sozo*. The context is obviously speaking of healing, or salvation in a *physical* sense. But notice what it is that the Lord responds to when He raises up the sick and heals him.

> And *the prayer of faith* will save the sick, and the Lord will raise him up. And if he has committed sins, he will be forgiven. (James 5:15)

Once again we see faith as the catalyst that releases the power of God. As we'll see more clearly as we go along, faith has to have a source. One cannot believe God for anything unless He has made His will clear in the matter, in the same way you cannot be positively sure what anyone else will do in a given situation unless you have their word on it. God's Word is our basis of faith. If we are expected to pray the "prayer of faith," there has to be a corresponding promise to *inspire* and anchor that faith.

It is true that in this case, the prayer of faith is prayed by the elders; older, more seasoned believers whose faith is presumably established in the truths of God's Word. Sometimes people get sidetracked in this passage because they get their eyes on the oil and the elders. I've said more times than I can count, "You can have enough elders to circle the block and enough Crisco to drown in, but if there is no prayer of faith offered, all you'll get is *greasy!*" It's not so much about the oil and the elders as it is the prayer of faith, and you can pray that prayer for yourself if you're grounded in the Word of God.

Nevertheless, this method of receiving healing is especially of value to those younger in the faith who may need the encouragement of trustworthy, seasoned, spiritual leaders praying for them. There's nothing better to inspire one's faith to receive from God than the assurance of trusted, proven spiritual mentors whose faith in the Word is rock solid.

Also, there is an obedience of faith involved here for one to receive healing from the Lord through the prayer of the elders. Over the years, many people have asked me to go and pray for a sick relative who, quite honestly, didn't want me or my prayer anywhere near them. I've learned that this verse isn't talking about that. We're not going to force God's blessings on anyone through our faith. God is not into "strong-arming" people into receiving from Him.

Calling for the elders of the church is an obedience of faith and an act of humility, both toward God and toward recognized spiritual authorities in the local church. The Bible is clear that "God resists the proud, but gives grace to the humble…" (1 Peter 5:5). When people reach out to God in faith and humility, God responds with power.

Some years back, when I was pastoring in New England, I had an experience along this line that was very illuminating. I received a call one day from an older couple in our church. The husband was calling on behalf of his wife because she was having severe back pain. At first, I started to do what we all too often do and said, "Yes, brother, we'll certainly be praying for her." After I hung up the phone, however, the Spirit of God checked me and brought James 5:15 to my mind.

He gently corrected me, telling me that they had done their part of James 5:14-15 by asking me, a recognized elder in their church and their pastor, to pray the prayer of faith for her healing. The only reason she hadn't called me herself was because she was in pain.

I called them back right away and asked if we could come over and pray for her, anointing her with oil. They were delighted at my suggestion and said they would love to have us come and pray. After arriving and solving the problem of finding some oil to use, we gathered in her room where she was lying on her bed, to pray the prayer of faith for her healing. We prayed and praised God for her healing because we *expected* God to do His part of "saving the sick" and "raising her up."

After we finished praying, we moved out of her room to give her a moment alone, and went into the spacious living room of their home to enjoy some of her artwork. After a moment, I happened to glance back into her room, and there she was, standing straight beside her bed, hands uplifted, praising the Lord. Her pain was gone, and we had a great testimony of God's faithfulness.

Due to my over-familiarity with ministry to the sick through the healing anointing and the laying on of hands, we almost missed this opportunity to see God's power released through His promise and the prayer of faith. Particularly during our years in traveling ministry, we primarily ministered to the sick through the healing anointing in conjunction with the word of knowledge. We had seen many people healed through those gifts of the Spirit working together. However, it's good to know that when there seems to be no special anointing present, there is power in the Gospel to heal when we simply believe.

God is not fickle or unfaithful to His Word. His salvation is not partial but complete. If we believe, we can see His power released to save *and* to heal!

Chapter 8

HEALING IN THE REDEMPTION

But He was wounded for our transgressions,
He was bruised for our iniquities;
The chastisement for our peace was upon Him,
And by His stripes we are healed. (Isaiah 53:5)

In this chapter, we want to plunge even deeper into the Gospel's power to heal. Healing is not a side issue of redemption, rather it is part and parcel of the redemption Jesus secured for us in His death, burial, and resurrection.

We still live in mortal bodies, meaning that they are still ultimately subject to physical death. We do not have the promise of living forever in these bodies as we have them now. For that matter, who would want to? I'm looking for a serious upgrade when the time comes!

Now this I say, brethren, that flesh and blood cannot inherit the kingdom of God; nor does corruption inherit incorruption. Behold, I tell you a mystery: We shall not all sleep, but we shall all be changed—in a moment, in the twinkling of an eye, at the last trumpet. For the trumpet will sound, and the dead will be raised incorruptible, and we shall be changed. For this corruptible must put on incorruption, and this mortal must put on immortality. So when this corruptible has put on incorruption, and this mortal has put on immortality, then shall be brought to pass the saying that is written: "Death is swallowed up in victory." "O Death, where is your sting? O Hades, where is your victory?" (1 Corinthians 15:50-55)

Thank God, one day we will receive a glorified body that is completely beyond death's reach. The Bible says that Jesus Himself "will transform our lowly body that it may be conformed to His glorious body" (Philippians 3:21), meaning that our glorified body will be like His resurrection body. This will be a body not restricted to the natural limitations our bodies have in their present form. What a day that will be!

What we *do* have a promise of now, however, is that God is still our Jehovah-Rapha, and that He will quicken our mortal bodies so that we might enjoy divine health. We each have a job to do and a race to run, and we don't need sickness and disease, the works of the devil, keeping us from fulfilling God's purposes for our lives.

We are going to examine the Gospel's power to heal and then look at scriptures that prove healing is in the atonement. For those of you who, like me, came from a different belief system regarding healing, I would just remind you to keep your heart open to receive fresh light from God's Word and check the Scriptures to see that the things we are teaching are true (see Acts 17:11).

> And when a violent attempt was made by both the Gentiles and Jews, with their rulers, to abuse and stone them, they became aware of it and fled to Lystra and Derbe, cities of Lycaonia, and to the surrounding region. And they were preaching the gospel there.
>
> And in Lystra a certain man without strength in his feet was sitting, a cripple from his mother's womb, who had never walked. This man heard Paul speaking. Paul, observing him intently and seeing that he had faith to be healed, said with a loud voice, "Stand up straight on your feet!" And he leaped and walked. (Acts 14:5-10)

The first couple of verses are simply setting up the scene for us. Paul and Barnabas are once again on the run, being pursued by both Jews and Gentiles who are outraged by their message. Having fled Iconium, they came to Lystra and Derbe. What's important for our purposes is to notice what they were doing there.

> And they were *preaching the gospel* there. (Acts 14:7)

What is the Gospel? It is the power of God to save, to deliver, and to *heal!* As Paul began preaching his message, it began to connect with one particular individual in the crowd. This man, a cripple from his mother's womb, had never walked a day in his life. Notice the effect that Paul's message had on this man.

> And in Lystra a certain man without strength in his feet was sitting, a cripple from his mother's womb, who had

never walked. This man heard Paul speaking. Paul, observing him intently and *seeing that he had faith to be healed…* (Acts 14:8-9)

There are a couple of very important things to notice at this point. First of all, for this man to have had "faith to be healed," Paul had to be preaching a Gospel that included healing, because "faith comes by hearing, and hearing by the Word of God" (Romans 10:17). You don't get faith for healing listening to someone preaching on the Antichrist and the Mark of the Beast! For this man to have had faith rising in his heart to be healed, it means that Paul was preaching a *healing Gospel!*

Secondly, Paul "saw" that the man had faith to be healed. He didn't have a supernatural revelation that faith was rising in this man's heart, rather he could simply see that the truth of the Gospel was taking hold and the expectation for healing was building in the heart of this crippled man. It's very obvious when faith begins to rise in the hearts of some people because it makes its way to their face! They light up and get excited! What Paul did next was crucial to the man receiving his healing.

Paul, observing him intently and seeing that he had faith to be healed, said with a loud voice, "Stand up straight on your feet!" And he leaped and walked. (Acts 14:9-10)

By now, having seen the principle of putting actions to our faith to release the Gospel's saving power, you can understand what Paul was doing. He was helping the man *act* on what he believed! The result was that the Gospel's healing power was released and the man was healed.

(Paul)....said with a loud voice, "Stand up straight on your feet!" *And he leaped and walked.*" (Acts 14:10)

Traditionally, we have done the same thing with this account as we have done with other such accounts. We attribute this miracle to special apostolic powers Paul had to do this, just as we similarly attribute Jesus' miracles to His divinity. In fact, many have a theology that miracles lasted until all the apostles of the first century died, and then they passed away. To believe this is like being the proverbial ostrich whose head is stuck in the sand to avoid seeing the obvious. There are more miracles of healing being performed today to confirm the Gospel's message than have ever taken place in the history of the Church.

Looking at this story carefully, and breaking down the sequence of events, however, makes it clear that Paul performed no miracle at all. Paul did three things to help the man receive his healing: 1) he preached the Gospel; 2) he saw the man had faith to be healed, and; 3) he told the man in a loud voice to stand up straight, on his feet. I'm sure his command to the cripple to stand was spoken in a loud, commanding voice to prompt the man to quick action before he could start reasoning himself out of his miracle with a long list of reasons why cripples can't walk.

The man himself was also instrumental in cooperating with the Gospel's healing power for his miracle. He too did three things that helped him receive his healing: 1) he heard the Gospel, 2) he had faith to be healed (meaning that he listened with an open and attentive ear), and 3) he acted on what he believed by leaping to his feet. Paul performed no miracle, as such, but simply preached the Gospel, which is the power of God to heal!

Had he the knowledge to act on what he believed without Paul's prompting, this man could have been completely healed before Paul even finished his message! This again underscores the importance of acting on what we believe to release the Gospel's saving power. This man sat there in Paul's audience with faith to be healed in his heart, but was absolutely no better until he put "feet to his faith," so to speak. It's not even clear whether the man knew he had faith to be healed or that his healing was just within reach until Paul prompted him to action.

This story in the book of Acts always reminds me of a story concerning a friend of mine who was healed of muscular sclerosis many years ago. When I knew Tom, he and his wife had preached the Gospel all over Russia, telling the testimony of his amazing healing to thousands throughout much of the former Soviet Union. But years before that, Tom was slowly dying from the debilitating disease that had stolen his vitality and caused him to go from being an active and vital person to being completely bedfast. Doctors had already warned his wife that the worst was still to come since he would need institutional care as his condition continued to deteriorate.

It was somewhere at this point in the story, however, that Tom heard the Gospel and was born again. Lying in what doctors said would be his deathbed, he thanked the Lord every night for the miracle of salvation, expressing that his only regret was that he had found the Lord at this point in his life and hadn't really had the opportunity to serve Him. Yet the Lord was still at work in Tom's life and got through to him that he didn't have to die of this disease.

The Lord directed Tom to begin reading the New Testament. As difficult as it was to do this with his MS, Tom began working through the New Testament, reading the miracles of Jesus and understanding more and more each day about God's will for him. After completing his reading of the entire New Testament, Tom asked the Lord what He would have him do now. "Read it again," was the answer he got, so he began at Matthew's Gospel and started through the New Testament again.

Having completed the New Testament for the second time, the Lord's direction to Tom was once again, "Read it again." Tom told me himself that it was on the third time through the New Testament that faith began to come. Tom didn't have anyone to direct him to the passages on healing or teach him about healing in the atonement. But the life-giving power of God's Word began to do a miracle in his heart and in his body.

Tom went from the deathbed to a wheelchair and began attending Bible school with his wife. At that time, the school had only a one year program, but the faith-building truths he learned there about God's *full* salvation bolstered his already growing faith. From the wheelchair, Tom went to a walker, growing in faith more and more each day.

Tom told me personally about the day that the Lord spoke to his heart; the day that would lead to complete healing in his body. By this time, he was using only a cane to get around and had begun to drive again. He had pulled his car to a stop at his home and was just finishing listening to a cassette tape of a message on the subject of faith before leaving his car, when the Holy Spirit spoke to his heart, saying, "Set your cane aside. You have faith to be healed." What I thought was truly amazing about this story, and what always connects it to this man who was healed as Paul preached in

Lystra and Derbe, was what Tom told me next. He said, "When the Lord told me I had faith to be healed, I didn't know that."

That so struck me, that one could have faith to be healed but not even know it. I wasn't sure how I felt about that at first, until I remembered the account of the man in Acts 14. Here this man also sat, still a cripple and unable to walk, with a heart full of faith to be healed. I'm sure that he was conscious of the excitement he felt as hope for a change to his life's circumstance rose in his heart, but without a knowledge of what was happening inside him or what to do about it, this man still sat there, unchanged by the Gospel. Unchanged, that is, until someone helped him to respond and *act* on what he believed!

I think this should again underscore our responsibility to help people arrive at a point of decision where they act on what they have heard. They need an opportunity to respond to the Gospel. We cannot assume that they'll just get it on their own. We need to present that opportunity to them so the power of the Gospel can be released in their lives.

What did Tom do with what the Lord said to him? He acted in faith on what the Lord said. He told me that when the Lord said this to him, his cane was more than a casual prop he had to use on occasion. As he would walk down the hallways at school, his motor skills were still affected, causing him to fall one direction, then another. He would use the cane to correct his balance and "steer" himself more or less in the direction he wanted to go. If someone stopped him to talk, he would have to lean on the cane to stand. If he stopped too long, he would have all his body weight supported with both hands on the top of the cane. This is where he was physically when the Lord said, "Set your cane aside. You have faith to be healed." The Lord knows what we do not.

This act of faith released the power of God and ultimately brought complete healing to Tom's body. When I knew him, as he and his wife would come to teach the Word for me in the church I pastored, I would never have known he ever had a serious, life-threatening illness. Whether the healing is immediate, as in the case of the cripple in Lystra, or gradual, as in Tom's case, the Gospel is the power of God to heal!

So, what is the Gospel of healing? What does the Bible actually say about the provision of healing for our bodies? Again, if Paul's message to the crowd in Lystra and Derbe caused faith to be healed to rise in the hearts of the hearers, that means Paul had to be preaching a Gospel that included God's redemptive provision for our bodies.

We have already seen that one of God's redemptive names is Jehovah-Rapha, "The Lord our Healer." This name stands alongside the other Jehovah titles as a revelation of God's redemptive disposition toward us, which was ultimately revealed in the provision Christ secured for us at Calvary. While no theologian would argue that He is still Jehovah-Tsidkenu, the Lord our Righteousness, or Jehovah-Shalom, the Lord our Peace, they often want to qualify God's healing graces, saying that such blessings were just for the Jews. But again, if we are going to say that healing doesn't belong to us, why don't we just say that *all* these benefits were just for the Jews of the Old Testament?

No, these names are God's self-revelation to us of His nature, His character, and His redemptive disposition toward us. The benefits these names revealed in the Old Testament pointed toward redemptive provisions that Christ would secure for us through His death, burial, and resurrection, as we have already seen.

There is no greater passage of scripture in the Old Testament to examine concerning Christ's atoning work on the cross than Isaiah 53. This chapter is a prophetic look at what Christ's death accomplished for us hundreds of years before it actually happened.

> Who has believed our report?
> And to whom has the arm of the Lord been revealed?
> For He shall grow up before Him as a tender plant,
> And as a root out of dry ground.
> He has no form or comeliness;
> And when we see Him,
> There is no beauty that we should desire Him.
> He is despised and rejected by men,
> A Man of sorrows and acquainted with grief.
> And we hid, as it were, our faces from Him;
> He was despised, and we did not esteem Him.
> Surely He has borne our griefs
> And carried our sorrows;
> Yet we esteemed Him stricken,
> Smitten by God, and afflicted.
> But He was wounded for our transgressions,
> He was bruised for our iniquities;
> The chastisement for our peace was upon Him,
> And by His stripes we are healed. (Isaiah 53:1-5)

While we will primarily look at verses 4 and 5 of this chapter, it is too beautiful a passage not to look at more of these verses which tell the greatest love story ever told, of a guiltless Savior who would take our guilt upon Himself to become the object of God's wrath, that we might be declared righteous in God's sight. This passage, particularly verses 4 and 5, reveal the comprehensive salvation that God made available to us in Christ's redemptive work. Most often, when talking about healing, people will point to Isaiah 53:5.

> But He was wounded for our transgressions,
> He was bruised for our iniquities;
> The chastisement for our peace was upon Him,
> *And by His stripes we are healed.* (Isaiah 53:5)

Here again, we see a full salvation for the total man. There is forgiveness of our sins to provide salvation by grace, peace for our soul (which answers the needs of our mind and emotions), and healing for our physical bodies – a complete salvation! In his own epistle, Peter refers to this passage when writing about Christ's vicarious death on the cross.

> Who Himself bore our sins in His own body on the tree,
> that we, having died to sins, might live for righteousness—
> *by whose stripes you were healed.* (1 Peter 2:24)

However, I believe that it is verse 4 that gives us a more complete message on the subject of healing in the atonement. The key is seeing it in the original Hebrew rather than in our English translations, as they do not tell the full tale.

> Surely He has borne our griefs
> And carried our sorrows;
> Yet we esteemed Him stricken,
> Smitten by God, and afflicted. (Isaiah 53:4)

At first glance, this might not seem to be a message on healing in the atonement (except perhaps in the most indirect way). Sickness does bring grief and sorrow, but that by itself would be slim scriptural evidence to establish healing in the atonement.

However, the Hebrew words translated "griefs" and "sorrows" are *kholee* and *makob* and should be translated "sickness" and "pains." Here are some places in the Old Testament where they are translated as such.

> And the Lord will take away from you all sickness (kholee), and will afflict you with none of the terrible diseases of Egypt which you have known, but will lay them on all those who hate you. (Deuteronomy 7:15)

> Also every sickness (kholee) and every plague, which is not written in this Book of the Law, will the Lord bring upon you until you are destroyed. (Deuteronomy 28:61)

> This is the writing of Hezekiah king of Judah, when he had been sick and had recovered from his sickness (kholee)... (Isaiah 38:9)

> Man is also chastened with pain (makob) on his bed, And with strong pain in many of his bones... (Job 33:19)

> Babylon has suddenly fallen and been destroyed.
> Wail for her!
> Take balm for her pain (makob);
> Perhaps she may be healed. (Jeremiah 51:8)

These examples show clearly enough that these same words, translated "griefs" and "sorrows" in Isaiah 53:4, should have been translated "sickness" and "pains." Many of the literal translations by some of our greatest Hebrew scholars have translated these words to reflect this idea.

> Surely our sicknesses he hath borne, And our pains—he hath carried them, And we—we have esteemed him plagued, Smitten of God, and afflicted. (Isaiah 53:4, *Young's Literal Translation*)

> But only our disease did he bear himself, and our pains he carried… (Isaiah 53:4, *Leeser's Translation*)

> Surely our sicknesses he carried, and as for our pains he bare the burden of them… (Isaiah 53:4, *Rotherham Emphasized Translation*)

While this scholarship is valuable in helping to confirm the true meaning of these Hebrew words, *kholee* and *makob*, we have an even stronger proof of their meaning. Matthew, writing years later about the healing ministry of Jesus, and under the inspiration of the Holy Spirit, quotes Isaiah 53:4 and leaves no question as to the meaning of these words and this verse.

> When evening had come, they brought to Him many who were demon-possessed. And He cast out the spirits with a word, and healed all who were sick, that it might be fulfilled which was spoken by Isaiah the prophet, saying:

"He Himself took our *infirmities*

And bore our *sicknesses*." (Matthew 8:16-17)

No one disputes the fact that Matthew is quoting here from Isaiah 53:4, as any center column reference in any reference edition Bible will confirm. But what's most important is that Matthew's use of Isaiah 53:4 leaves no question that the context of the verse is *Christ's bearing of our sicknesses and pains on the cross*. Matthew's use of this verse during Christ's earthly healing ministry is simply showing that these healings came on the basis of the redemption Christ would provide through His death on the cross. Whether these benefits were administered before or after Jesus actually died is not an issue, since in the mind of God, Christ was "the Lamb slain from the foundation of the world" (Revelation 5:8).

Again, healing is part and parcel of the redemption. Christ's bearing of our sicknesses was not some separate act from His dying for our sins. Sickness and disease is a physical result of the spiritual death that Adam introduced into man's experience through his sin. As some have said, "Sin is the *root* and sickness is the *fruit*." When Jesus died, totally satisfying our debt before God, balancing the scales of divine justice, He released us judicially from the affects of sin physically *and* spiritually, temporally *and* eternally.

Another thing to observe in the lines of Isaiah 53:4 are the verbs translated "borne" and "carried." They are the Hebrew words *nasa* and *sabal,* and both carry the meaning of "bearing something as a punishment or chastisement." These same words, describing Jesus' bearing of our sicknesses and pains, are also used in this same chapter to describe His bearing of our sins as well.

By His knowledge My righteous Servant shall justify many,
For He shall bear (sabal) their iniquities. (Isaiah 53:11)

And He was numbered with the transgressors,
And He bore (nasa) the sin of many... (Isaiah 53:12)

Again, the use of these verbs to describe both Jesus' sacrificial bearing of our sins and our sicknesses prove that when He died as our substitute to pay the full penalty for our sins, He provided both forgiveness for our sins and healing for our bodies. As David said in Psalm 103:3, "Who forgives all your iniquities, Who heals all your diseases..." This dual benefit is often called the "double cure" and is underscored in passages where the twin benefits of forgiveness and healing are seen to go hand in hand, as in James 5:14-16 and others.

> Is anyone among you sick? Let him call for the elders of the church, and let them pray over him, anointing him with oil in the name of the Lord. *And the prayer of faith will save the sick, and the Lord will raise him up. And if he has committed sins, he will be forgiven. Confess your trespasses to one another, and pray for one another, that you may be healed.* The effective, fervent prayer of a righteous man avails much. (James 5:14-16)

Having seen how Jesus' death paid the full penalty for sin and released us from its power, it should be easy to see why both forgiveness and healing would come together when faith is exercised toward God. We can preach with great confidence then that the healing of our bodies as well as the forgiveness of our sins, is available through the redemption of Jesus Christ.

Chapter 9

SEEING THE GOSPEL'S HEALING POWER AT WORK

Good news from far away is like cold water to the thirsty.
(Proverbs 25:25, NLT)

The reality of the Gospel's healing power really came home to me years ago when a door to television ministry in India opened for us. Healing had always played a significant role in my life and ministry since God spoke to me as a very young man, telling me that part of my assignment as a minister would be to stand for the truths of healing in the Word of God. Years later, I would have the opportunity to publish a book on the subject, *Healing: The Gospel Truth* (Jubilee Press, 1995).

Our website regularly attracted the attention of pastors and leaders from other countries who often wanted American ministers to come and bring the Word to their people. Like many American pastors, I had many invitations to go and share the Word in conferences and churches in other parts of the world. As one who loves missions, it was always a very tempting opportunity, but my responsibilities in our own church at home kept me busy, and it never seemed right until I was contacted by a ministry in the city of Nagercoil, in Tamil Nadu, India's southernmost province.

While I wasn't able to accept their initial invitation to come and preach for them, I suggested that we keep in touch. Some months later, they asked if I would be interested in supplying programming for their local Christian channel. I was hugely interested! We began sending them programming at once.

Now when I say "television ministry," I'm sure you have something different in mind than what it actually involved. The idea of Christian television in our country is often accompanied by images of elaborate set decoration and huge production budgets. In light of this, it is really quite laughable to remember our modest early efforts at "international television ministry."

We found a little round table in our house, and I sat at it while teaching. For my backdrop, we purchased one of those stand up dividers with a Corinthian column-like design on it. I don't think that first camera was even a production quality camera, but merely a simple home video camera. My oldest son, now twenty-one, was very young at the time, and we assigned him the job of pointing the camera in my general direction and hitting the record button. If you had looked in the dictionary for the word "rinky-dink," I think it would have had a picture of our set next to it, illustrating the meaning of the word!

But powerful things often come in humble packages. After all, even the Savior of the world made his début in a manger! We edited those first broadcasts, all of which were on the subject of divine healing, sent them off to India, and waited to see what God would do. It took a while, but the testimonies began to find their way to us. Some took a while because our friends in India had to find time in their very busy ministry schedule to translate them from Tamil into English.

However, some of the testimonies came directly to my own email address, which I gave out each week on the show. One of the earliest ones is still one of the most powerful to me, and I will share it here. (Please note that I have tried to leave this and the other testimonies I will share as close as possible to how they were sent to me. Only minor grammatical errors were corrected to make their meaning flow more smoothly.)

> *Dear Sir,*
>
> *I do not know how to address you, as I come from a Hindu family. I heard little about Jesus Christ and never believed much of his miracles.*
>
> *I used to make fun of people that they were cured by Jesus Christ. I was sick and in bed and I was changing my TV channel. There was not much interesting thing on television and I got annoyed and was changing the channels as mad man, but in few minutes it did not work.*
>
> *To my surprise, I saw someone (I saw your name and email at the end of the show) was telling about Christ and he can heal anyone. I was stunned as I was having pain on my knees and could not walk for weeks.*
>
> *But when the prayer was offered to Jesus to heal the sick people, I said, "Jesus, heal me." When you finished the offering of*

prayer to Jesus I felt a great touch from someone and I saw a hand took me out of my bed and made me to walk. I thought it was dream. But it is 4th day and I am walking without any pain on my knee.

I saw your email at the end of the show and I thought of sending my gratitude to you. Now what must (I) do? Is there anyone here that can help me to know what I have to do? I offer prayer that Jesus works through you. I am expecting a reply soon.

Your friend
Ponraj

Words cannot express the excitement I felt in seeing God take our humble efforts and use them for His glory. It was neither a well-known healing evangelist, nor the virtue of some anointing I possessed as I laid hands on and prayed for Ponraj that raised him up. The power inherent in the Gospel made Ponraj whole!

I immediately responded to the email address he had used, sharing with him how to make Jesus the Lord of his life. I also directed him to our friends in India, who lived close enough for Ponraj to get to their ministry base. Soon after, I received this email from him.

Respected Sir,

I am much excited getting an email from you on the other side of the world.

I am really believed you have the blessing of Jesus and his power is with you. Your prayer and Jesus healed me. I thank Jesus hundred times. I worshipped many gods for healing for my illness and no cure. But only you prayed in Jesus and I got healing. That is wonderful. You are so kind to offer prayers for sick people.

Last Sunday, I went to the place you sent the address. They were so much happy you directed me to them. One of the esteemed person(s) called Pastor Kulanthaivelu and others treated me so well and told me about you and your service to mankind in India. I bow to you for loving our country to cure the people and tell them the happy news of healing.

At this place they asked me to call Jesus to forgive my sins so I can be his son. It was really something new for me. I told them you sent me a prayer similar to theirs. They offered a wonderful prayer for me and I felt something funny inside of me but that is alright.

Now I trust in Jesus. They asked me to come to their place (to) know more of Jesus. I will go there often.

I say prayer to God. God Jesus bless you.

Your servant in Jesus,
Ponraj

Reading this testimony now, it is almost embarrassing to see how many times this humble man tried to credit me and our small efforts for his healing. Yet traditionally, we have done the same thing by crediting Paul and others for the healings that were actually accomplished through the power of the Gospel, when people simply believed. We should be encouraged by knowing that we have the same Gospel, and it has never lost its power to totally transform the lives of those who will believe.

Ponraj's testimony was only the first of many that found its way to us over the years. Many times, I have pulled out these stories of the Gospel's healing power to encourage myself and show others how the Word of God is inherently empowered by God to save, deliver, and heal. Here are some other favorites of mine.

Dear Respected Sir Randy Bunch,

In God's name, I write to you. I am Mrs. Ganapathy, a home maker. I do not know computer but my daughter Devi knows.

This is the first letter I ever wrote to anyone. I did not write even to my own family so far because we are raised in a strict Hindu family. We are not allowed to talk to strangers. We do into look into other men.

You may think, why I write this letter to you. I am writing this for one good reason. My mother had eye problem in her left eye and we spent large money for her hospital expenses. But no doctor was able to cure her. She had lost her sight in the left eye.

My mother likes to watch television and she was changing the channel. She tried to change in to other but the remote was not working and you were speaking. My mother called my daughter (her grand-daughter) and asked her what is the preaching about as she was curious to see a white man saying something which caught her attention. My daughter was translating for her with her little knowledge.

But we got the message. We heard that Jesus can heal the sick. So my mother, my daughter and myself prayed to Jesus to heal her left eye.

It was so marvelous. After you said prayer to Jesus, my mother said she saw Jesus touching her, though she did not have any idea about Jesus. She was healed instantly. Now she has vision in her both eyes and she quit watching other TV programs and likes to watch yours every time.

We all thank you, thank Jesus. Do you have any picture of Jesus so we can keep and worship Him? We do not know anything about Jesus and how to offer or say or ask Jesus.

So inform us as what we must do.

With folded hands we give our thanks from our hearts.

Faithfully,
Ganapathy Sivasamy
Odayakulan, Cbr
India

I have been watching Pastor Randy (on) Kingdom TV for the last 2 months and it gave me to increase my faith. I have a brother who has mental problem for 8 years. He was taken to many doctors, but no result. He was like a child and we had to do everything for him like feeding, bathing, dressing, and so on.

When I was watching Pastor Randy's message on healing, I brought my brother near the TV. When he was praying for the sick I also prayed with him and put my hand (on him) and prayed for him. I did not see any change at that time. But the next morning he was sitting quite and was brushing his teeth. He talked normal after 8 years.

We all shed tears thanking the Lord and Pastor Randy for brining healing and joy to our family.

Jesus, bless Pastor Randy
Kuppusamy, Punnai Nager.

My daughter Jasmine was admitted in the hospital for brain fever. She was suffering with much pain. The doctors gave drips but it seemed she was in great agony.

We used to record your healing messages that come on Kingdom TV. So we have decided to play your message in the hospital so she and we all can hear and increase our faith to heal her. We brought the TV, VCR and played your message and we all knelt down and prayed when you started praying for the sick.

As soon as we finished the prayer we saw our daughter opened her eyes and was praising. Not only that 2 other patients in adjacent room also were healed from their illness. Thanks to you and God. God bless you Pastor for your love for the sick people.

James, Neyyoor

This next one was from our friend we called Velu (his real name was much longer and hard for us to pronounce). He was one of two brothers who headed up the ministry in India which gave voice to our healing messages to people in their area. Though I have lost touch with Velu and his brother, Elan, they will always be very dear to our hearts.

Dear Pastor Randy,

Trust that you got my earlier email. The Lord is working and we have people calling and letters keep coming.

Just now a lady came and told that she heard you were preaching about a woman with an issue of blood. This lady had the same problem and she was abandoned by the doctors and she became very, very weak (and) fragile.

Almost she hated to live as she thought she was a burden to her family. When she (she is Hindu) heard that the woman had 12 years of issue of blood problem, she turned the volume high and was listening. After the message when you prayed, she without her knowledge knelt down and (was) shouting to Jesus for her healing.

She said it was so powerful that she felt a touch and immediately she was cured from the problem. She is Hindu and it is not easy for her to testify like this but she did. She wanted me to write this to you.

Great things are happening. Tell the church that they (are) reaching the people that they never ever (would be) able to reach. We thank you for reaching our country and also thanks to your church and other sponsors...

See you in April. Bless you.
Love,
Velu

There is nothing new under the sun. People experience the same problems today that they did when Jesus ministered here on earth. The Gospel is able to meet any and every need, regardless of the century and regardless of the country.

My 7 month old grandson was suddenly affected by diarrhea and was unconscious. We all were scared and took him to the hospital. The doctor treated him but said he was not sure if he would be cured without any complication.

Since I am a regular viewer of Kingdom TV and watch your messages. I went home to hear your message on the evening as it was scheduled on that day. My whole family cried and joined with you when you prayed for the sick.

When we returned to hospital we saw he was healed and was playing. The doctor said it was miracle and said surely God only healed him. Thank you Pastor Randy for the wonderful healing prayer.

God bless you.
Mrs. Sugunabai, Ethavilai

I had diabetic problem and the doctors took me to amputate my leg from the knee. I was prepared to this surgery. I was about to go to the hospital on June 16th.

One of my friend(s) gave me a CD (the format they use in India is VCD instead of DVD) of Pastor Randy's message that was telecasted through Kingdom TV. I watched with my family and we trusted that Jesus could help me too.

We all prayed with tears for healing my wounds in the leg. The next day, when the doctors checked, they said there is no need for amputation and can be cured with injections.

I thank God and Pastor Randy.
Mohanraj, Punnaivilai

Some of the testimonies we received were not mere healing testimonies, but testimonies of deliverance from demonic influence and possession. Again, these underscore the power of Gospel over all the works of darkness.

I am a Hindu and I did not know much about Jesus. My family and me were tormented by the evil spirits almost every day. When the evil spirit came upon me, I did not know what I was doing. I used to beat my wife and children. All my income disappears just like that.

While I was having my tea at (a) small shop I saw the TV there and heard someone was telling about Jesus and what he can do. I said to myself, if Jesus is real God, I want him to help me to (be) delivered from evil spirits. When I said that I felt a lightening upon me and I was delivered. Now my family and I am doing fine.

I was told that it was a man of God named Rev. Randy from America.

Murugesan, Thandikkarankonam

I don't share these stories to in any way to shine some undue light on the role we played during this season of ministry. As I said before, our efforts were laughable compared to the standards of most modern television ministries. The point is that even from the most primitive of platforms, the power of the Gospel can shine through to save, deliver, and heal. The Gospel is truly the power of God unto healing!

Chapter 10

THE GOD WHO SEES AHEAD

And Abraham called the name of the place, The-Lord-Will-Provide (Jehovah-Jireh); as it is said to this day, "In the Mount of the Lord it shall be provided." (Genesis 22:14)

We have seen that the Gospel is God's power to save. His provision for us is comprehensive, covering every need of our lives. So far, we've focused primarily on spiritual and physical salvation, but we must cover at least one other area before we close this teaching on the Gospel's saving power: God's material provision and deliverance from lack.

Perhaps nothing is more controversial in the Church today than the message of prosperity. Wars both large and small have been fought over whether or not God wants to bless the believer materially. While there have been extremes taught on the subject of prosperity, one would have to ignore enormous portions of the

Word of God to deny God's desire to abundantly supply the needs of His children.

> And you shall remember the Lord your God, for it is He who gives you power to get wealth, that He may establish His covenant which He swore to your fathers, as it is this day. (Deuteronomy 8:18)

> The Lord is my shepherd;
> I shall not want. (Psalm 23:1)

> Who is the man that fears the Lord?
> Him shall He teach in the way He chooses.
> He himself shall dwell in prosperity,
> And his descendants shall inherit the earth.
> (Psalm 25:12-13)

> Oh, fear the Lord, you His saints!
> There is no want to those who fear Him.
> The young lions lack and suffer hunger;
> But those who seek the Lord shall not lack any good thing. (Psalm 34:9-10)

> I have been young, and now am old;
> Yet I have not seen the righteous forsaken,
> Nor his descendants begging bread. (Psalm 37:25)

> For the Lord God is a sun and shield;
> The Lord will give grace and glory;

No good thing will He withhold
From those who walk uprightly. (Psalm 84:11)

Therefore do not worry, saying, "What shall we eat?" or "What shall we drink?" or "What shall we wear?" For after all these things the Gentiles seek. For your heavenly Father knows that you need all these things. But seek first the kingdom of God and His righteousness, and all these things shall be added to you. (Matthew 6:31-33)

And my God shall supply all your need according to His riches in glory by Christ Jesus. (Philippians 4:19)

Beloved, I pray that you may prosper in all things and be in health, just as your soul prospers. (3 John 2)

Again, regardless of how we might want to meet the needs of our own children, our love and care for them could never exceed God's love and care for His children. How could his love somehow fail to encompass meeting the *material* needs of His children when even we would do as much?

If you then, being evil, know how to give good gifts to your children, how much more will your Father who is in heaven give good things to those who ask Him! (Matthew 7:11)

The Bible clearly teaches that the things that happened to natural Israel in the Old Testament serve as types and examples to us. Moses serves as a type of Christ, our deliverer. The blood of the Passover Lamb serves as a type of the blood of Christ, which delivers us from the judgment of God. The Red Sea crossing serves as a type of water baptism, separating us from the world, and so on (see 1 Corinthians 10:1-11). When the children of Israel came out of Egyptian bondage, God met their every need. He was not only their Healer, established by His covenant name, Jehovah-Rapha (as we saw earlier), but He was also their provider.

> Forty years You sustained them in the wilderness;
> They lacked nothing;
> Their clothes did not wear out
> And their feet did not swell. (Nehemiah 9:21)

If you study the journey of the children of Israel from Egypt to the Promised Land, you'll see that it is filled with one provisional miracle after another by the hand of God, meeting their every need. Water spewed forth from rocks, manna fell from the sky, and quail were supernaturally "herded" through their camp to feed their desire for meat. Even in their disobedience and rebellion, God took care of their natural needs while they were on their way to an even *better* provision in the Promised Land. This land would be the ultimate in material provision and blessing, especially to a people who had just come out of slavery and bondage.

> ...and that you may prolong your days in the land which the Lord swore to give your fathers, to them and their descendants, "a land flowing with milk and honey." For the land which you go to possess is not like the land of Egypt from which you have come, where you sowed your seed and watered it by foot, as a vegetable garden; but the land which you cross over to possess is a land of hills and valleys, which drinks water from the rain of heaven, a land for which the

Lord your God cares; the eyes of the Lord your God are always on it, from the beginning of the year to the very end of the year. (Deuteronomy 11:9-12)

In fact, when the spies Moses sent into the land returned, they brought back samples of the fruit of the land, including one cluster of grapes so large it had to be carried between two men on a pole.

These obvious pictures of abundance and blessing show us God's care for His children in the Old Testament and prefigure for us His redemptive provision for our material needs in Christ (Philippians 4:19). It makes no sense to say that God would abundantly bless His *servants* in the Old Testament but not His *children* in the New Testament, who live under "a better covenant, which was established upon better promises" (Hebrews 8:8).

Another irrefutable argument for God's desire to abundantly bless and provide for His children is the connection made throughout the Scriptures between obedience and blessing. In the Law, God's blessings were contingent on the people obeying His commandments (see Deuteronomy 28:1-14), and in the book of Proverbs, prosperity and increase come to those who act wisely, demonstrate integrity, and give generously.

Since we know that God wants us to obey Him, act wisely, demonstrate integrity, and give generously to others, it stands to reason He must want us to be blessed! In Deuteronomy 28, the curse of the Law (Deuteronomy 28:15-68), which includes every kind of poverty and calamity imaginable, comes to those who *disobey* God's commands. They don't come to those who love God as some form of "spiritual discipline" to make them more holy or teach them lessons on patience or piety.

Above all these arguments, however, is the fact that the redemption of Jesus Christ is clearly shown in the New Testament to include provision for our material needs. In speaking to the Corinthian church about money, Paul tells us how Jesus, in His redemptive work, became poor that we might become rich.

> For you know the grace of our Lord Jesus Christ, that though He was rich, yet for your sakes He became poor, that you through His poverty might become rich. (2 Corinthians 8:9)

Now before you rush to say, "Well now, brother, this was speaking of Jesus being made poor so that we could be made rich *spiritually*," ask yourself, "If that is so, why did Paul use it in the context of money?" Notice the setting in which Paul tells us of Christ being made poor for us. Let's look at it in a contemporary translation that helps the meaning to be clearly seen.

> So we have urged Titus, who encouraged your giving in the first place, to return to you and encourage you to finish this ministry of giving. Since you excel in so many ways—in your faith, your gifted speakers, your knowledge, your enthusiasm, and your love from us—I want you to excel also in this gracious act of giving.
>
> I am not commanding you to do this. But I am testing how genuine your love is by comparing it with the eagerness of the other churches.
>
> You know the generous grace of our Lord Jesus Christ. Though he was rich, yet for your sakes he became poor, so that by his poverty he could make you rich. (2 Corinthians 8:6-9, NLT)

Jesus did not become poor spiritually. In what way could a man who lived a perfect, sinless life be called *spiritually* poor? Jesus, however, did leave His home and position in Heaven to be born into the most humble circumstances imaginable. He became a man and experienced life in all its reality as we do, experiencing every test and temptation we could ever face, and He did it without sinning. He faced betrayal and rejection, and ultimately died the death of a criminal that we might be exalted and seated together with Him in heavenly places (see Ephesians 2:4-6).

In dying for our sins and paying the penalty that divine justice required, He leveled the death blow to the root of all poverty and lack. Now the way to God's abundant provision is made available that we might requisition Heaven's resources to carry out the call and commission He has given to the Church.

Now we can partner together with His purposes in the earth through giving and receiving, which is His plan for bringing financial and material blessing into our hands. As we do, and as we grow in the grace of giving, we are to experience increase that we might continue to be a channel of blessing to others.

Remember this—a farmer who plants only a few seeds will get a small crop. But the one who plants generously will get a generous crop. You must each decide in your heart how much to give. And don't give reluctantly or in response to pressure. "For God loves a person who gives cheerfully."

And God will generously provide all you need. Then you will always have everything you need and plenty left over to share with others.

As the Scriptures say,

"They share freely and give generously to the poor.

Their good deeds will be remembered forever."

For God is the one who provides seed for the farmer and then bread to eat. In the same way, he will provide and increase your resources and then **produce a** great harvest of generosity in you.

Yes, you will be enriched in every way so that you can always be generous. And when we take your gifts to those who need them, they will thank God. So two good things will result from this ministry of giving—the needs of the believers in Jerusalem will be met, and they will joyfully express their thanks to God. (2 Corinthians 9:6-12, NLT)

Notice verse 8 in the *Amplified Bible*.

And God is able to make all grace (every favor and earthly blessing) come to you in abundance, so that you may always and under all circumstances and whatever the need be self-sufficient [possessing enough to require no aid or support and furnished in abundance for every good work and charitable donation]. (2 Corinthians 9:8)

God is a good farmer. He's the one who made the natural laws which reflect spiritual reality (see Romans 1:20). No farmer plants a crop expecting to only get back the seed he originally planted. He'd be better off to just eat his seed! No, just like an expectant farmer, as we give with an obedient and generous heart, God will see to it that we experience increase both personally and in the fruit of our giving to others.

> Give, and it will be given to you: good measure, pressed down, shaken together, and running over will be put into your bosom. For with the same measure that you use, it will be measured back to you. (Luke 6:38)

This is not to say that there are not many potential snares when dealing with money. We must always be wary of covetousness and realize that financial assets require diligent stewardship as well as integrity of heart. Many are the heartbreaking stories of ministries and businesses that lost all they had gained through greed and mismanagement. The Bible is filled with admonitions to guard our hearts and see to it that we are above reproach when dealing in financial matters. This is why God has no "get-rich-quick" schemes, and prosperity only really increases in our lives as we mature and learn to be better stewards, both of our own resources and of God's.

Nevertheless, none of these admonitions to be good and wise stewards should make us think that God is against us prospering financially. Indeed, He wants us to mature and grow that we might become faithful stewards of His resources.

> Beloved, I pray that you may prosper in all things and be in health, *just as your soul prospers.* (3 John 2)

No doubt there are those better equipped than I to teach on the subject of financial prosperity and blessing, but I want to share how God's gracious provision was revealed and expressed in my own life at a time when it looked like things could go very much the wrong way for me. In fact, it is when we are at our worst that God shows Himself as the very best!

It happened just as I was, unbeknownst to me, about to enter a new chapter in my life. During a time of prayer, God told me to be ready to "serve Him in a different capacity." I didn't really know what He meant, though I had been seeking Him about certain matters in my life. He also spoke to me and assured me that He would provide for me in this next season. As God said to me, "I will provide for you," the words, "I have seen ahead" came into my mind at the same moment. He was saying that He had seen ahead to where I was going and that He would make provision for me. It took a few moments for me to make the connection between these two things, "making provision" and "seeing ahead," but then the Holy Spirit brought it all back to my remembrance in one powerful moment.

Not long before that, I heard one of my favorite Bible teachers sharing on the story of Abraham when he was told by God to sacrifice his only son, Isaac, on one of the mountains of Moriah (Genesis 22). This is the story in which another of God's Jehovah titles is revealed; Jehovah-Jireh, "The Lord Who Provides" or "The Lord our Provider" (Genesis 22:14).

As Isaac and his father made their way to the place where Abraham would have to sacrifice his only son, Isaac asked his father where their sacrifice was. Abraham answered his son saying, "My son, God will provide for Himself the lamb for a burnt offering" (Genesis 22:8). This was Abraham speaking his faith in God's provision as well as a prophetic foreshadowing of Christ one day being offered up as God's sacrificial Lamb for the sins of the whole world. A footnote in the *New American Standard Bible* brings out the literal meaning of the word translated "provide" in this verse. It is to "see."

If you know the story, you know that God did just as Abraham believed He would. As Abraham was about to plunge the knife into the bosom of his only son, Isaac, the Angel of the Lord stayed his hand and showed him a ram caught in the thicket. Abraham had proven his faithfulness to God, and God provided a substitute for Isaac, just as He provided Christ to be the substitute for each of us on another hill on another day. Abraham offered that sacrifice to God that day and named the place Jehovah-Jireh, "The Lord will Provide" (see Genesis 22:1-14).

In fact, the literal meaning of Jehovah-Jireh is, "The Lord will see." In the footnote of the *World English Bible*, the name Jehovah-Jireh is also rendered, "Yaweh-Seeing." Notice some other translations of Genesis 22:14.

And he called the name of that place, The Lord seeth. Whereupon even to this day it is said: In the mountain the Lord will see. (Genesis 22:14, *Douay-Rheims*)

Avraham called the place Adonai Yir'eh [Adonai will see (to it), Adonai provides] — as it is said to this day, "On the mountain Adonai is seen." (Genesis 22:14, *Complete Jewish Bible*)

And Abraham called the name of that place Jehovah-jireh: as it is said to this day, In the mount of the LORD it will be seen. (Genesis 22:14, *Webster*)

These translations, along with others, indicate that the name carries the idea that the Lord sees or will see. Even our own English word "provision" is a compound word, from *pro*, "before," and *vision*, "to see" and means "to see ahead." After all, you cannot make provision if you cannot see ahead and anticipate the need.

There's no doubt that, since all the Jehovah titles have redemptive implications, the idea of Jehovah "seeing" had to do with Him looking ahead to the sacrifice of Jesus, which is the source for all of God's provision for us (Romans 8:32). But to Abraham it had a more immediate meaning, as it did to me when God spoke to me.

You have to think of Abraham as he made his way on that three day trek to the mountain. All he knew was that God had commanded him to offer his son as a sacrifice on the mountain. Since God had told him that it would be through Isaac that his descendents would come, he knew that if necessary, God would raise him from the ashes of that sacrifice (see Hebrews 11:17-19). Nevertheless, I have to imagine it was the longest three days in Abraham's long life.

However, what he couldn't see was that while he made his way toward the mountain, there was a ram making his way up that same mountain. God had seen the need ahead of time and was already preparing the provision to be at the right place at the right time. In our lives when we wonder how God will be able to get to us what we need when we need it, we need to remember that He is the God who *sees ahead* and is already working on what we need so that it's there just when we need it.

When God spoke to me and said that He had seen ahead and would provide for me, I had no idea that I was about to go through the biggest life change I would ever experience up to that time. In a few short months, I had left my ministry, moved across country, and started what amounted to a brand new life. But even in the midst of what might have seemed like chaos to others, God was there, making a way and providing for our needs.

For twenty-two years, I had done little but full-time ministry and felt ill-prepared for a career in the secular world. What skills I did have had always been used to do the work of the ministry. And while I knew the "gifts and calling of God are irrevocable" (Romans 11:29), and that I would one day be in ministry again, I had no idea how long that might take. I needed a job, and God was right on time with the right job to both meet my needs and give me experience in dealing with people from a different angle than I had experienced in all my years of ministry.

God's provision for me was not merely adequate, but abundant, as the employment He provided for me paid a higher salary than any I had ever made before. Though this job would not be where I would ultimately serve Him, it was wonderful to see His faithfulness to me during a season when life posed so many challenges.

During this time, I was able to forge the relationships and connections that became a part of the new life into which He graciously brought me. I grew to understand that being a minister is not just about preaching and pulpits but about serving people in their place of need and pain, and sharing out of the treasury of my heart the things God deposited there through my years of walking with Him. During all the time away from the pulpit, I never lost my sense of connection with Him or my sense of calling. Rather, I learned to use what He has given me in a different way. Truly, His grace was and is sufficient.

Chapter 11

OUT OF A HORRIBLE PIT

I waited patiently for the Lord;
And He inclined to me,
And heard my cry.
He also brought me up out of a horrible pit,
Out of the miry clay,
And set my feet upon a rock,
And established my steps.
He has put a new song in my mouth —
Praise to our God;
Many will see it and fear,
And will trust in the Lord. (Psalm 40:1-3)

As we close our study on the Gospel's saving power, I just want to give one final admonition: Realize the great work of redemption that has been done for you, at great cost, and embrace it wholeheartedly, with both arms. Don't let anyone or anything rob you of the inheritance that God has provided for you in Christ Jesus.

The Bible says, "The entrance of Your words gives light; It gives understanding to the simple" (Psalm 119:130). Those who have not received, or who have shut out light on the truths we've discussed simply cannot see them. It is like one who has been invited to a great banqueting hall which is completely dark. Though the food has been set and the feast is ready, the guests cannot partake of what they cannot see.

As light comes to you from the Word, the blessings on God's banqueting table of redemption are illumined and you can partake. However, to those to whom the light has not been shown, the banqueting hall is still dark. They are ignorant of the feast, in spite of the great expense that has been paid to make the provision available. Many have been talked out of the blessings they have plainly seen through the light of God's Word simply by listening to those who have never seen (and perhaps even refuse to see), all that God has provided for them.

Also, there is the devil. He is real, and he will do all he can to make you feel inadequate to partake of the feast God provided for you. He will point out your missteps and misdeeds, telling you that you are unworthy to receive the grace of forgiveness and partake of God's banquet. Many have the mistaken idea that God will not lift us out of a pit of our own digging, but the whole history of God's dealings with Israel was Him lifting them out of pits of their own digging. Indeed, the plan of redemption carried out through the manifold wisdom of God, was God lifting man out of a pit of his own digging.

We've seen that the Gospel is the power of God unto salvation. God saves through His Word. Time and time again in my life, when I needed help, it was the Word of God that lifted me. No matter where we find ourselves in life, regardless of how far we might have strayed from His path for our life, there is always a way back.

> Fools, because of their transgression,
> And because of their iniquities, were afflicted.
> Their soul abhorred all manner of food,
> And they drew near to the gates of death.
> Then they cried out to the Lord in their trouble,
> And He saved them out of their distresses.
> He sent His word and healed them,
> And delivered them from their destructions.
> (Psalm 107:17-20)

How did God save? What was the lifeline that He threw to the one drowning in his own folly? It was the Word. That is how God saves. I am not alone in having run the gambit of trying to get God to respond to my need by every other means than the one He has designated. I have begged, pleaded and pouted, but in the end, it was getting back on the Word and trusting what He said that brought me through. His Word will do the same for you.

The fact of the matter is, this isn't just about you and me getting what we need from God. Jesus said, "Freely you have received, freely give" (Matthew 10:8). You cannot give away what you have not received, and you cannot share what you do not know. The world is waiting, whether it knows it or not, for a people who will demonstrate the life-changing power of the Gospel and proclaim it from a heart full of conviction.

May we ever say with Paul, "For I am not ashamed of the Gospel of Christ, for it is the power of God unto salvation for everyone who believes."

PRAYER FOR SALVATION

Having presented you with these truths concerning the comprehensive salvation God has provided for you, we would be remiss if we did not offer you the chance to make Jesus Christ the Lord of your life. We want to invite you to act on what you've heard and be born again.

If you believe Jesus died for your sins and was raised from the dead to justify "all who call upon His name," simply pray this prayer from your heart. Again, it's not the combination of the words that matters, but the communication of your heart's faith to God.

Dear Heavenly Father,

I believe you sent Jesus into the earth to die for my sins and for the sins of the whole world. I believe He died for me and that You raised Him from the dead, and that He is now seated at Your right hand, ready to save all those who call upon His Name. I do so now.

I ask you, Jesus, to come into my heart and life and make me brand new. I surrender my life to your Lordship and receive the gift of eternal life you made available through your sacrifice. Jesus, You are my Lord.

Father, thank You for saving me.

In Jesus' Name, Amen.

If you prayed that simple prayer, we'd love to hear from you and help you in any way we can to grow in your walk and relationship with God. Email us at info@nlc-paso.org and we will pray for you and with you to see God's purposes realized in your life. God bless you!

Notes

[1] C.I. Scofield, D.D., *The New Scofield Reference Bible* (Oxford University Press, Inc., 1967), page 1211.

[2] C.I. Scofield, D.D., *The New Scofield Reference Bible* (Oxford University Press, Inc., 1967), page 1211.

ABOUT THE AUTHOR

Randy Bunch has been a minister of the Gospel for over thirty years, beginning his preaching career as a mere seventeen-year-old boy in his hometown of Taft, California. Since then, Randy's ministry has moved in a number of directions. He has pioneered churches on both coasts and traveled extensively throughout the Unites States and abroad, teaching and preaching the Word and ministering in the power of the Spirit.

The gifts of the Spirit have always played a significant role in Randy's ministry, particularly in regard to healing. He has even authored a book on the subject, *Healing: The Gospel Truth*. For a number of years, between pastoring churches, Randy traveled throughout the United States conducting "Holy Ghost Meetings" which were characterized by the Spirit of God confirming His Word with signs following. In later years, through his television broadcasts in India, Randy was privileged to see many healed from a wide range of maladies by the power of God. To him, the testimonies from this season of ministry are still some of the great highlights of the healing ministry.

As a pastor, it is Randy's great desire to see every believer connected to and equipped for God's purpose for their life. The Church must be mobilized, motivated, and equipped to touch their world, both near and far, if the lost are to be reached and discipled. For this reason, there is a strong emphasis at *New Life Church of Paso Robles* on discipleship and equipping the believer to take his or her place in the Body of Christ.

Randy is a graduate of Rhema Bible Training Center in Broken Arrow, Oklahoma and holds a Masters in Theology from Life Christian University in Tampa, Florida. He lives in Southern California with his wife, Maria, and their children. For more information on the ministries of *New Life Church of Paso Robles*, simply go to their website, at www.nlc-paso.org.